SHEFFIELD
in the
1930s

PETER HARVEY

Sheaf Publishing ● *in association with The Star*

First published in 1993 by Sheaf Publishing Ltd., 35 Mooroaks Road, Sheffield 10, in association with The Star.

Copyright:Peter Harvey, Sheffield Newspapers and Sheaf Publishing.

ISBN: 1 85048 014 1

For permission to use photographs, or for help in obtaining them, my thanks to Mr Bert Dagg, Mrs Evelyn Smith, the Archives Department of John Lewis Partnership, the Local Studies Department of Sheffield Libraries, Mr Michael Marsden of Marsden's Caterers of Sheffield Ltd., Mrs. Valerie Hartshorn, Mr Peter Chapman, the Grimsby Evening Telegraph, and Dr. Derek Haydn Taylor. All the other photographs are from the files of the The Star or from my own collection.

Peter Harvey

SHEFFIELD NEWSPAPERS have always been fond of taking photographs of enormous bits of metal produced by one or other of the local firms. Sometimes they were crankshafts, sometimes boiler drums, and they were often photographed on the backs of huge lorries, holding up lots of traffic on their way from Sheffield to somewhere else.

This one is slightly different. It is (I am assured) a main entablature girder weighing 46 tons, part of a 6,000 ton high-speed forging press, made by English Steel Corporation Ltd., in 1932. Happily, it isn't holding up any traffic because it is being pushed along a railway line by a very pleasant little saddle tank steam engine. It is also being very closely watched by a man in a bowler hat.

The author, with his mother, Handsworth, 1935.

Sheffield in the 1930s

A YOUNG GIRL was asked to leave Glossop Road Baths, Sheffield, in 1930 because her swimming costume did not conform to the regulations. It was supposed to be one-piece and black. It was one-piece, but it was coloured. Her mother caused a ruction over the incident and a week later the Baths Committee changed its rule and allowed coloured costumes. By 1936, the rule still applied that all swimming costumes had to be one-piece, and even men had to have their upper halves covered.

A woman complained after being warned by one of the attendants at Millhouses open-air pool because she was wearing a two-piece costume. Men and women were allowed to mix in the water at Millhouses, but not when they sunbathed. Men had to sit on the grass on one side of the pool, women on the other, and iron railings kept them apart, although they were allowed to talk to each other through the railings. Presumably the committee felt that the extremely low temperature of the water at Millhouses would prevent any shenanigans when they swam together.

These restrictions were not part of the Victorian or Edwardian eras. They were still in force in the late 1930s and they are within the memory of people who are still alive in the 1990s.

The thirties are often characterised as the time of festering unemployment, war jitters, the talkies, airship disasters, the abdication, art deco, Noel Coward, the means test, Penguin paperbacks, the Spanish Civil War, Busby Berkeley dance routines, and so on. They were also the last decade of enforced black swimsuits and iron railings between men and women sunbathers.

It was predominantly a time of depression, and for a manufacturing city like Sheffield that meant severe unemployment. In 1930 the city had 43,000 people out of work. By 1931 the total had risen to 59,000 and it hovered around 60,000 for the next few years. Sometimes there was a scramble for jobs. When a firm on The Moor advertised for a lorry driver in December 1930, more than 100 men turned up to apply, and some of them stormed the premises shouting that they wanted work.

There were worse scenes five years later, when 10,000 people attended a demonstration

Looking up Fargate in the mid 1930s, with Cole Brothers still at Coles' Corner.

Middlewood Hospital, the new admission block for the South Yorkshire Mental Hospital, opened February 1935.

in Town Hall Square to protest at cuts in unemployment payments. The City Council, in session at the time, refused to meet a deputation from the protesters, who then charged the Town Hall gates. All the entrances were locked and police reinforcements were called in. Rocks and sticks were thrown, nine policemen and several demonstrators were injured and there were more than twenty arrests before order was restored. Full unemployment payments were restored the next day, but simmering discontent about the so-called transitional benefit and the hated means test continued.

There were well-intentioned local efforts to try to help the employment situation. The City Council instigated schemes, usually road building, that were intended to provide work, but even these were hampered. In June 1930, Sheffield's Lord Mayor, acting on behalf of all the municipal corporations, told the Cabinet that work schemes for the unemployed were being held up by Government bureaucracy, the grants were too low, and not enough money was being spent. It made little difference. Later in the year a Sheffield Trade Mission went to South America to try to drum up orders.

Cole Brothers ran a Sheffield Week every year, displaying and promoting Sheffield-made goods. The Rotary Club, backed by the City

Council, ran a Spending for Employment campaign to try to encourage people to spend more especially on locally-made items. But it was none of these things that eventually eased the unemployment problem. By the last two or three years of the decade, all eyes were on Herr Hitler (as he was still called). Britain started to prepare for war. As it did, Sheffield's unemployment problem subsided, and was ultimately wiped out. But at an awful cost.

Less gloomily, it was the era of the talkies. One by one local cinemas converted to talking pictures. And new cinemas opened – the *Capitol*, the *Carlton*, the *Forum*, the *Plaza*, the *Rex* and the *Ritz*. The *Hippodrome*, Cambridge Street, and the *Royal*, Attercliffe (reborn as the *Regal*), were converted from theatre to cinema. The *Albert Hall* and the *Theatre Royal* burned down, the *Playhouse* staggered from financial crisis to financial crisis, and *Attercliffe Palace* had a patrons' bar for the first time in its history.

On the sporting front there was an almost unbelievable situation in 1990s terms, in which Sheffield Wednesday reached the final of the FA Cup in 1935 (and won it) and Sheffield United reached the final in 1936 (but lost); Sheffield had a baseball team, the Sheffield Dons, playing in the Yorkshire Baseball League (with Sheffield United goalkeeper Jack Smith at first base), and national boxing champion, Johnny Cuthbert; greyhound racing started at Owlerton and Hyde Park; and cricket still graced Bramall Lane during the summer months.

In 1938, the possibility of war rose to a probability. During the Czechoslovakia crisis of that year gas masks were issued in Sheffield, trenches were dug in parks and on recreation grounds, and anti-aircraft guns and searchlights were set up around the city. The crisis passed, but from then on air raid precautions were taken more seriously. The Chief Constable and members of the Chamber of Commerce climbed Wincobank Hill one night to see how much of Sheffield's industry could be seen in darkness. Test black-outs were held in August and October 1938 and RAF planes flew over to see how effective the black-out was.

Anderson air-raid shelters arrived and were sent out to householders, only a few at first, but by the end of 1939 there were nearly 60,000 in the city. Repeated campaigns were mounted to recruit more volunteers for the A.R.P. (Air Raid Precautions) and other civil defence services. 'Sheffield is not ready' was the slogan. Ready or not, war was declared on 3rd September 1939 and on the two days before the declaration thousands of women and children were evacuated from the city. In retrospect, the last four months of 1939 seem to belong more to the 1940s than the 1930s. Sheffield, along with every other community in the country, waited nervously for the worst to happen. And hardly anything happened at all. It was the so-called Phoney War, the calm before the storm.

The motor car, hitherto a novelty and an apparent boon, had developed into a major problem by the thirties. In 1930, seventy people were killed in road accidents in Sheffield and nearly 1,500 were injured. Parking was virtually unrestricted, and traffic congestion was a major issue. In efforts to cope with the motor car, Belisha beacon pedestrian crossings were introduced in 1934, the 30 miles-an-hour speed limit (some people wanted an even lower limit) and compulsory driving tests were both introduced in 1935, and a bewildering variety of new traffic schemes were tried in Sheffield city

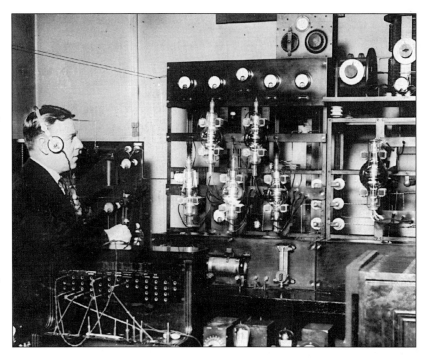

centre. But the death toll and congestion continued.

A road census carried out in 1935 showed that the city's busiest road, The Wicker, was used by 11,127 motor vehicles, 729 horses, 7,030 cyclists and 3,279 tram cars on an average day. A former Corporation transport committee chairman predicted that at some time in the future Sheffield would build a tunnel, like the Mersey Tunnel, from Moorhead to Waingate, to keep through traffic out of the city centre. If he could see what has happened since then he would be rotating in his resting place.

Politically, it was a volatile period. At the General Election of 1931, the Tories won all

The transmitter of Sheffield's first radio station, 6FL, was in Corporation Street. By the end of 1932 the transmitter was closed down, but a studio remained, first in Castle Street, then back in Corporation Street.

Sheffield's first consignment of Anderson air raid shelters – 150 of them – arrived at the LNER's Bridgehouses goods station on March 2, 1939. About 50 were built on recreation grounds and in parks as demonstration models for the public. The rest were sent out to householders. The shelters photographed here, on the Arbourthorne estate, may be some of them.

Sir Oswald Mosley, the British Fascist leader, was a regular visitor to Sheffield in the years leading up to the Second World War. A branch of his party was formed in the city in May 1931. At one meeting, in 1934, a large crowd gathered in Barkers Pool and booed and shouted as Mosley and his black-shirted followers marched into the hall two abreast. About 400 police were on duty around the hall and after scuffles broke out, six men were detained. There was more trouble inside when Mosley's speech was interrupted, and leaflets were thrown from the grand circle. Several men were ejected by stewards.

At another meeting in May 1935, when this photograph of Mosley was taken backstage, more violence was expected. The Communist party organised a counter-meeting in Holly Street and a religious speaker addressed another crowd nearby. But extra police were on duty and this time there was no fighting.

seven Sheffield seats, gaining five from Labour. Labour lost heavily in local elections too; six City Council seats in 1930, eight in 1931, and the two they lost in 1932 meant that they lost control of the council. But not for long. They won back six seats and regained control the following year, and in the General Election of 1935 they won back four of the city Parliamentary seats.

Women started to play a fuller part in public life. Sheffield had its first woman alderman on the City Council in the 1930s, and its first woman Lord Mayor, who broke the ancient tradition of the Cutlers' Feast being a males-only shindig, and was the first woman Lord Mayor to attend a Coronation. Sheffield Business and Professional Women's Club was formed. The woman who captured most attention during the decade, however, was a young graduate of Sheffield University, Amy Johnson, who was acclaimed for her solo flight to Australia. She returned to Sheffield to give a talk at the Victoria Hall.

It was also the time of the wireless. By the mid-thirties one in seven of the population of Sheffield had a wireless licence and the number was rising every year. A licence then cost ten shillings (50p) and listeners had a choice of two programmes, National and Regional. Among

the items they could hear were *In Town Tonight* which started in 1933 and went on for twenty years, *Scrapbook*, *Monday Night at Seven*, which later became *Monday Night at Eight*, and, of course, the long-running *Children's Hour*. One of the most famous radio programmes of all time, *ITMA*, (It's That Man Again) starring Tommy Handley, started very quietly (and with little acclaim) in July 1939.

A new pest emerged – the person who turned his wireless set up to full volume and then sat out in his garden with the windows and

doors wide open listening to it. Judging by letters to the editor columns in local newspapers of the time, there were other pests too, people whose motor cycles, motor cars, and various items of electrical equipment caused interference on other people's wirelesses. There was nothing quite like a bit of wireless interference to inspire an irate letter.

One of the interesting aspects of researching this period is to see how the use of certain words has changed. Headlines on Monday morning newspaper wedding reports invariably included an adjective no sub-editor would dare use today. 'Gay turn-out at Fulwood wedding', they said. Gay still meant happy then. 'Breeze at Sheffield council meeting', the headline said, using the word breeze to mean vociferous argument. The shorter, harder word 'row' has replaced breeze in this context. 'Singular turn of events at Darnall', they said. Singular, meaning unusual, is another word that has dropped out of the headline writer's vocabulary.

One of the sadder aspects of researching the period is seeing how many marvellous news pictures of the time have not survived. There was a photograph of an airship passing over High Street. I would like to have included it here, but it has gone. I have traced only one surviving photograph of King George VI and Queen Elizabeth's visit to Sheffield in 1937, and that a rather ordinary group photograph taken inside the Town Hall. I know there was a much more interesting picture of the Royal couple

waving from the Town Hall balcony but I have not been able to find it. Nor could I find photographs of the Sheffield Dons' baseball team, the escaped tiger at the *Empire Theatre*, Winston Churchill at the City Hall, the Salvation Army soup kitchen that toured poorer areas of the city (here again, I know one was taken), Amy Johnson on her visit to the Victoria Hall, the English women's soccer team and the visits to Coal Aston by Sir Alan Cobham's Flying Circus.

There was a delightful picture taken during the Silver Jubilee celebrations of 1935. It showed a Sheffield street party with revellers holding a large sign telling the rent man to stay away because they had spent the rent money on their celebrations. I have seen it in microfilm files, but the original print is lost. The list of losses is enormous. There was even a photograph of men and women talking to each other through the iron railings that used to separate them at Millhouses Park swimming pool. But it too has disappeared.

Jordanthorpe Hall, Old Norton, was one of several large houses aquired by the Corporation in the 1930s. At the time of buying it, in 1932, the city fathers were unsure of whether to use the land for housing or an aerodrome.

One of Cole Brothers' 1930s delivery vans.

January

1   Arthur Ponsonby, MP for Brightside, became a Baron in the New Year Honours.

4   Jimmy Dunne, Sheffield United centre forward, scored four goals for the second match running when United beat Leicester City 7-1.

25   St Alban's Church, Darnall, consecrated.

February

1   Psalter Lane Methodist Church opened.

6   Alderman F. Marshall (Lab.) won a parliamentary by-election at Brightside caused by the elevation of Arthur Ponsonby.

24   The Cinema House showed its first talking picture – Climbing the Golden Stair.

     The 50-cwt statue of Queen Victoria was removed from Town Hall Square and re-erected at Endcliffe Park.

28   A new Girl Guides' HQ opened in the Mappin Buildings, Norfolk Street.

March

5   A Sheffield Wednesday-Nottingham Forest match was delayed for nineteen minutes because the Forest team coach broke down three times on its way to Sheffield.

7   Test run of the first diesel-engined bus in Sheffield.

10   The Abbeydale Cinema started showing talkies.

24   The Adelphi Cinema started showing talkies.

26   Last meeting of Sheffield Guardians.

April

1   Sheffield Union Hospital changed its name to the City General Hospital.

---

3   Wilson Road Synagogue formally opened by Mr Lionel N. de Rothschild, lay-head of the Anglo-Jewish community.

7   Ivor Novello's first visit to Sheffield, in Symphony in Two Flats at the Empire.

22   By beating Derby County 6-3, Sheffield Wednesday won the First Division championship for the second consecutive season.

24   Fitzalan Market closed.

25   Castle Hill Market opened. (Official opening, May 9).

28   Chantrey Picture House started showing talkies.

May

5   Wicker Picture Palace started showing talkies.

14   The Baths Committee lifted its ban on coloured swim suits at city baths.

24   Miss Mercedes Gleitze swam for 36 hours at Glossop Road baths, setting a new British endurance record.

29   Bents Green open air school officially opened.

June

3   Eastbank House, Sheffield diocesan babies' home, officially opened.

5   A new one-way traffic scheme started along Surrey Street, Norfolk Street and Union Street. Only trams allowed to go directly from Fargate to Moorhead.

10   The Lord Mayor suggested that Sheffield should have a municipal orchestra.

18   Widespread thunderstorms; three houses badly damaged by lightning at Attercliffe.

1930

27   Sheffield Corporation printing works, Scotland Street, opened by Earl Russell.

July

5   Viscount Plumer, Sir Hugh Bell, John Galsworthy and Sir Henry Hadow given honorary degrees by Sheffield University.

7   Manor Community Association formed.

17   Longley Council School opened by Alderman E. Snelgrove.

22   Arnold Reynor appointed director-producer of Sheffield Repertory Company in place of Maxwell Wray, who went to Birmingham rep.

24   Firth Park branch library opened by Lord Ponsonby, the first new library in Sheffield for 24 years.

28   A.V. Alexander, MP for Hillsborough and First Lord of the Admiralty, became the first cabinet minister in the world to broadcast

---

Sharrow Grange was converted into the Workshops for the Blind, and opened in October 1930.

on TV, at the Baird Studios, Long Acre, London.

The Conservatives, the Citizen's Party and local manufacturers decided to form a new municipal party – the Progressive Party.

August

9   A Blackburn Bluebird aeroplane given to Sheffield Flying Club by Mr George Kenning.

13   Holy Trinity Church consecrated as the new parish church of Millhouses.

20   Meeting held to form a gliding club in Sheffield.

22   Johnnie, aeroplane belonging to Amy Johnson, on show at Cole Bros.

25   Workshops for the Blind, Sharrow Lane, opened for work. Formal opening October 23.

September

3   Sheffield Aviation Week; passenger flights over the city and displays of stunt flying.

4   Concord Park presented to Sheffield by Alderman J.G. Graves.

18   First trials at Owler Bar of Sheffield Gliding Club's new glider.

(It crashed two days later at the club's first meeting)

27   British Home Stores' shop opened on The Moor, the company's first in a northern provincial city.

30   Chamber of Commerce decided to send a deputation to the City Council to press for an aerodrome for Sheffield.

October

5   A Sheffield man was among six people who survived the crash of the airship R101 in France.

7   Mr Percy Boswell Brown, deputy chairman, Hadfields Ltd., installed as Master Cutler.

14   The Bishop launched an appeal for 1,000 guineas to build churches on new housing estates.

25   S. and E. dairy, Archer Road, opened.

November

1   Labour lost six seats at the municipal elections, five to the Progressives, one to an Independent Liberal.

10   Alderman Harold Jackson elected Lord Mayor.

20   Prince George visited Sheffield University and opened the new Royal Infirmary casualty block.

22   Freedom of the city conferred on Mr J H Scullin, Prime Minister of Australia.

23   Castlegate opened to traffic.

December

9   Sir Alan Cobham, the well-known aviator, was retained by the City Council to advise on the possibilities of an aerodrome.

13   Sheffield Wednesday beat Birmingham 9-1 at Hillsborough, creating a new scoring record for the club.

15   Sheffield's first public wash house opened in Daniel Hill.

The last troops – a battery of the Royal Field Artillery – left Hillsborough Barracks in February 1930. They had only been in Sheffield four months. Before that the barracks had been empty for some time. When they pulled out the buildings were unoccupied for two years. In October 1932, the War Office put the barracks up for auction but after a top bid of £10,000, they were withdrawn. A month later it was announced that Mr H.M. Burdall, head of Burdall's Ltd., manufacturing chemists, had bought the barracks for use by his firm.

1931

January

11 General Edward J. Higgins, head of the Salvation Army, spoke at the Citadel and at the Regent.

17 Burgess, of Sheffield Wednesday, scored his 100th goal for the club in a 4-1 win over Grimsby Town at Hillsborough.

February

18 Announcement that an ice rink with accommodation for 5,000 spectators was to be built on Ecclesall Road, opposite Thompson Road. (It was not built).

22 Owlerton Stadium taken over by a new group.

24 Methodist Congress opened at the Victoria Hall.

26 Burngreave Council School officially opened.

March

11 Edgar Wallace, the thriller writer, opened a Liberal bazaar at the Montgomery Hall.

31 Thos. Firth and Sons Ltd. and John Brown and Co. Ltd. merged.

Sheffield Repertory Company reported a profit for the first time, without help from grants, gifts or guarantees.

April

1 Mr E.B. Gibson appointed Town Clerk of Sheffield.

16 First production by the Excelsior Players, John Walsh Ltd.'s amateur dramatic society, at the Chalet Theatre, Kenwood Park.

17 Jimmy Seed, of Sheffield Wednesday, appointed manager of Clapton Orient.

20 England opening batsmen Herbert Sutcliffe and Percy Holmes made personal appearances in specially-erected nets on the first floor of Walsh's store.

May

4 Alf Strange, of Sheffield Wednesday, chosen to captain England against France and Belgium.

7 A Sheffield branch of Sir Oswald Mosley's New Party was formed at a meeting at the Grand Hotel.

Alderman C.W. Gascoigne told a conference that Sheffield had some of the worst slums in the north of England.

17 A new traffic control system started in Town Hall Square, with signals controlled by a policeman from a kiosk in the the centre of the square.

20 Woodhouse branch library opened.

25 Serre Memorial Park and Shelter, France, dedicated to Sheffield men killed in the First World War, was opened.

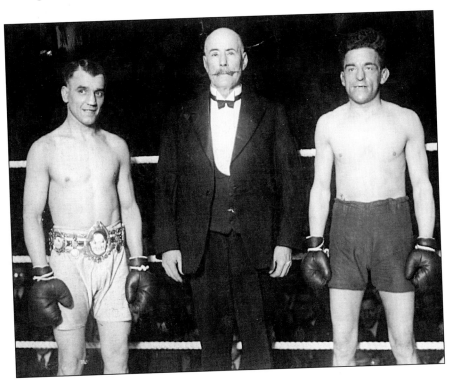

Pride of Sheffield, Johnny Cuthbert, left, poses with his opponent Frank McAloran and referee Nat Mawby, of Nottingham, before a fight at Edmund Road Drill Hall in April 1931. Cuthbert, then British featherweight champion, knocked out McAloran, former Irish featherweight champion, in the seventh round. It was his first fight in Sheffield for two and a half years and a crowd of 5,000 filled the hall to watch it.

Cuthbert lost his featherweight title to Nel Tarleton later in the year, but the following year moved up a weight and won the British lightweight title which he held till 1934 when he was beaten on points by Harry Mizler. Over ten years he had about 250 fights. The Lonsdale Belt he is wearing on the picture was awarded to him in 1930.

June

6 The Hippodrome Theatre, Cambridge Street, closed. (It re-opened as a cinema on July 20).

13 The Gloops Holiday Home for Children opened at Mablethorpe.

18 St Vincent's Church, Solly Street, consecrated. It had been open for 80 years but consecration was delayed till it was free of debt.

27 Longshaw estate was handed over to the National Trust.

July

6 Sheffield Cathedral was struck by lightning during a severe storm.

18 Lord Burghley, English and Olympic hurdles champion, competed in Hallamshire Harriers' sports at Bramall Lane.

27 Education Committee agreed to abolish means-testing for free places at King Edward VII School.

One of Sheffield's best known High Street shops, Boots the chemists, was given a complete new frontage in October 1931, with a wider entrance and a canopy over it. This is how the frontage looked before it was remodelled.

August

1 Outer Circle bus route (25 miles in one hour fifty minutes, for a fare of 1s 3d – about 6p) started.

10 Sheffield Mail merged with the Yorkshire Telegraph and Star.

September

5 Sheffield Wednesday scored seven goals against Bolton, making a total of 17 goals in the first three matches of the new season.

19 A pencil drawing called Standing Nude, by Eric Gill, was withdrawn shortly before the opening of Sheffield Society of Artists' annual exhibition at the Mappin Art Gallery. The gallery chairman said he did not think it was suitable for public exhibition.

22 Capt. P. J. Sillitoe, Chief Constable of Sheffield, appointed Chief Constable of Glasgow.

Mr Walter Hedley K.C. appointed Recorder of Sheffield.

October

1 Amy Johnson gave a talk at the Victoria Hall on her solo flight to Australia.

6 Mr Joseph Ward, chairman of Thos. W. Ward Ltd., installed as Master Cutler.

8 General Jan Smuts was given an honorary degree by Sheffield University.

16 Boots the Chemist's High Street shop re-opened after rebuilding and extension.

23 Opening of Montague Burton's new store at the junction of Attercliffe Road and Staniforth Road.

November

2 Labour lost eight seats in the municipal elections but retained control of the City Council with an overall majority of two.

9 Alderman T.H. Watkins installed as Lord Mayor.

12 Princess Mary visited Vickers' works and opened Sheffield Chrysanthemum Society exhibition.

24 Paderewski gave a recital at the Victoria Hall.

December

2 Mr Neil Porter became new director-producer of Sheffield Repertory Theatre.

7 Dr. Hugo Eckener, pilot of the German airship, Graf Zeppelin, made a private visit to Sheffield, staying with Mr P.R. Kuehnrich, of Holly Court, Ecclesall.

30 Supt. R. Hall, of West Bar Police, chosen to be Chief Constable of Rotherham.

Abbeydale Hall was bought by Norton Rural Council in March 1931 for use as council headquarters. The council had been short of offices and a meeting place for several years. The hall's new use did not last long. Three years later the old rural district was taken over by Sheffield and the rural council ceased to exist.

Owlerton Stadium, photographed by night in January 1932, when greyhound racing started. According to one report, the stadium offered racing 'under conditions which cannot be obtained on any other track outside London.' The club, with its wide expanse of window front and cosy seating, was a great attraction, it said, and the tote was 'a mechanical and electrical marvel'.

1932

January

5 A petition signed by 23,000 people asked that the name of the new public hall in Barkers Pool should be the Memorial Hall. (After lengthy debate, the City Council decided to call the building the City Hall, but named one of the halls inside it the Memorial Hall).

12 Greyhound racing started at Owlerton Stadium, with 10,000 people at the first meeting.

14 Because of the price of gold, speculators toured Sheffield buying sovereigns and half-sovereigns.

29 Cole Brothers' sixth annual Sheffield Week started, with all 26 display windows devoted to Sheffield-made goods.

February

9 Report that the number of people charged with drunkenness in Sheffield, per thousand population, was the lowest in the country in 1930.

10 Inaugural lunch of Sheffield Publicity Club.

March

11 A £100,000 appeal was launched to mark the centenary later in the year of the Royal Hospital.

18 C & A's new store in High Street opened.

21 A loss of more than £300 on the year's working caused anxiety about the future of Sheffield Repertory Company.

April

1 A prehistoric stone implement was found during excavations on the Wybourn estate.

12 Southey Green Council School opened.

20 A set of wrought iron gates from Hayes Park Place, Kent, was given by Mr Charles Boot for the main entrance at Concord park.

23 Mr John Nicholson, secretary of Sheffield United Cricket and Football Club for 33 years, was knocked down and killed by a lorry near the Midland Station as he was on his way to join the United party for a match at Birmingham. (About 6,000 people attended his funeral at Darnall the following week).

29 Wisewood Council School opened.

30 Bents Green Methodist Church opened.

May

7 LNER locomotives, including the so-called 'hush-hush', No. 10000, and the Pacific, Royal Lancer, went on display at Victoria Station.

21 A new Wesleyan Reform Church opened at Richmond, built in six months on the site of an older chapel removed for road widening.

June

2 Our Lady of Beauchief Roman Catholic Church, Woodseats, opened.

10 Mr J.E. Davison, manager of Chesterfield F.C., was appointed secretary-manager of Sheffield United.

25 Stanley Baldwin, leader of the Conservative Party, was chief speaker at a Conservative fete at the Farm Grounds.

Banner Cross Hall was bought by Mr Charles Boot for the use of his firm, Henry Boot and Sons Ltd., in 1932.

July

8 Sir Alan Cobham gave flying displays at Coal Aston and took the Lord Mayor on a flight over the city.

18 Mr Charles Boot bought Banner Cross Hall for the use of Henry Boot and Sons Ltd.

30 An All-England ladies soccer team beat a team of French ladies 4-2 at Abbeydale Park.

August

4 Laurel and Hardy, the film stars, visited Sheffield and made personal appearances at the Cinema House.

9 The Post Office issued a booklet explaining Sheffield's new postal district numbering.

27 A plane belonging to Sir Alan Cobham's Flying Circus crashed near spectators at a flying gala at Coal Aston. The pilot was seriously injured.

September

4 The new Jewish Burial Hall and Cemetery at Blind Lane, Ecclesfield, was consecrated.

22 The City Hall was officially opened.

24 Roberts Brothers' store on The Moor re-opened after extensive rebuilding of the frontage.

26 Louis Armstrong, 'the World's Greatest Trumpeter', opened at the Empire for a week with his New Rhythm Band.

27 A letter to a local newspaper said the stone lions on the City Hall stage ought not to be there because they did not harmonise with the rest of the decorations.

October

3 Alderman J.G. Graves gave another 37 acres of land, laid out as a golf course, as an addition to Concord Park.

4 Lt. Col. Arthur Neale Lee, director of Walker and Hall Ltd., installed as Master Cutler.

10 Jimmy Dunne, Sheffield United centre forward, scored all four goals in United's 4-2 win over Sheffield Wednesday, a record personal score for matches between the two clubs.

26 Christopher Stone, 'gramophone record recitalist' (the early name for a disc jockey) played records for an audience of 3,000 at the Victoria Hall.

November

1 Labour lost overall control of the City Council in the municipal elections. After the count, Labour had 46 seats, Progressives, Conservatives, Independent Liberals and Independents had 49 between them.

9 The engagement is announced of Mr (later Sir) Bernard Miles and Miss Josephine Wilson, who met while in the acting company at Sheffield Rep.

Alderman Ernest Wilson installed as Lord Mayor.

14 Hillsborough Barracks were bought by Mr H.M. Burdall, head of Burdall's Ltd., manufacturing chemists. The barracks had been offered for sale by auction in October and withdrawn at £10,000.

26 Graham's furniture store, The Moor, opened.

December

6 An anonymous gift of £650 helped ease Sheffield Repertory Company's financial problems.

8 Yehudi Menuhin, 15-year-old violin prodigy, gave a concert at the City Hall.

31 Sheffield Repertory Company launched an appeal for £10,000 to pay off their mortgage and recondition their Townhead Street theatre.

First meeting at Hyde Park greyhound track.

— NEW CITY HALL. SHEFFIELD —

January

2　Sheffield Wednesday had a record attendance (65,345) for their match against Arsenal at Hillsborough.

5　Very Revd A.C.E. Jarvis installed as Provost of Sheffield.

12　The City Hall organ formally opened by Sir Edward C. Bairstow, Organist and Master of Music at York Minster.

February

3　Cole Brothers launched a Home and Civic Week with special displays throughout the store, 'to give people a pride in their city'

6　A Salvation Army mobile soup kitchen started touring poorer areas of Sheffield, offering free soup and vegetables at a penny a portion.

24　Heavy snowstorm lasted almost continuously for 48 hours, causing widespread damage and traffic disruption.

March

13　Former Prime Minister David Lloyd George addressed a meeting in the City Hall.

23　Sir Henry Coward conducted his farewell concert with Sheffield Musical Union.

A new footbridge over the railway at Woolley Wood, built to replace a surface crossing on which three young girls were killed a few years before, was opened in May 1933.

April

6　Prince George opened Sheffield Corporation's new electricity generating station at Blackburn Meadows.

30　Five houses were struck by lightning in Sheffield.

May

6　First of several performances of a dramatised version of Hiawatha at the City Hall.

28　Sheffield became the first city to have its name inscribed in the Jewish Golden Book.

June

7　Mr H.S. Newton appointed Chief Education Officer for Sheffield.

14　Alderman J.G. Graves elected a Town Trustee.

24　The Lord Mayor inaugurated a Sheffield Week organised by the Junior Chamber of Commerce.

28　Sir Percy Greenaway, Lord Mayor of London, drove through Sheffield in his state coach, opened High Storrs Secondary School and attended the Forfeit Feast.

Sheffield motor cyclist Bill Beevers went to the Isle of Man for his first Tourist Trophy race in 1933 — and crashed in practice. The experience did not deter him. He went on taking part in TT races up to the 1950s, winning more replicas than any other rider. Bill started out working as a locomotive fireman, then converted his hobby into a business and became a motor cycle dealer in 1937.

July

3　Cllr. Luther Milner elected president of the Wesleyan Reform Union at its annual conference in Sheffield.

5　The City Council decided to convert the Nether Edge route from trams to buses.

10　Blacka Moor, given to Sheffield by the Graves Trust, was opened by the Lord Mayor.

11　House of Lords approved Sheffield's plan to take over Norton Rural District.

August

3　The City Council accepted an offer from the Graves Trust to build a children's playground at Attercliffe Recreation Ground.

1933

An ox was roasted at Abbeydale Park annual charity gala, with ox roast sandwiches at sixpence each, in aid of Sheffield Poor Children's Seaside Holiday Fund.

Sheffield Newspapers organised an outing to Croydon Aerodrome for a large party of readers.

26 The British Hospitals' Air Pageant at Coal Aston Aerodrome attracted about 15,000 people to watch six hours of flying.

September

7 Wisewood Senior School opened.

12 Two-way traffic resumed in Pinstone Street.

St Aidan's Church, Park, consecrated.

October

3 Mr Charles John Walsh, general manager, United Steel Companies Ltd., installed as Master Cutler.

4 Sheffield's rates cut by sixpence in the pound.

18 Mr Walter Runciman, president of the Board of Trade, chief guest at the Cutlers' Feast.

23 Mr Jan Bussell appointed producer of Sheffield Repertory Company.

26 Sheffield Musical Festival, revived after a break of 22 years, included four concerts in two days at the City Hall.

November

1 Labour regained control of the City Council in the municipal elections by gaining six seats, five from the Progressives, one from the ILP.

2 Alderman J.G. Graves gave £16,000 to rebuild and enlarge Weston Park Museum.

9 Alderman Fred Marshall elected Lord Mayor.

Dr. J.K.M. Rothenstein appointed director of Sheffield Art Galleries.

23 The Graves Trust presented Tapton Court to the Royal Hospital for use as a nurses' home.

31 It was announced that the Bishop of Sheffield's 100,000 Guineas Appeal had succeeded – raising more than 107,000 guineas.

December

2 A tiger escaped from its cage at the Empire Theatre, injured an attendant and was at large for four hours.

8 Mr Billy Walker, former England and Aston Villa footballer, was appointed manager of Sheffield Wednesday.

14 The Prince of Wales visited Sheffield as part of a country-wide tour organised by the National Council of Social Service to see work being done for unemployed people.

TOWN HALL SQUARE AND FARGATE, SHEFFIELD.   C.537.

1934

January 1934

11 St Polycarp's, Malin Bridge, consecrated.

18 Appeal launched to save Sheffield Repertory Company.

23 LMS locomotive Royal Scot on show at Midland Station.

February

2 Now 90,728 wireless licences in Sheffield, said a report — one for every seven of the population.

9 Alderman J.G. Graves gave Sheffield University £15,000 to build a students' union.

10 Between them, Hallamshire Harriers and Sheffield United Harriers won three team and two individual titles at the Yorkshire Cross Country Championships.

17 A fifth-round FA Cup tie between Sheffield Wednesday and Manchester City attracted a crowd of 72,841 people, a new record attendance for Hillsborough. The match was drawn 2-2, Wednesday's 17th consecutive match without defeat — another club record.

March

1 Sir John Simon, Foreign Secretary, addressed a mass meeting at the City Hall.

14 Norton Association for the Prosecution of Felons celebrated its 150th anniversary.

23 Woolley Wood School was opened.

25 Buses replaced trams on Nether Edge route.

26 Trumpeter Louis Armstrong appeared at the Empire Theatre for a week.

April

4 Cllr. Mrs Grace Tebbutt elected Sheffield's first woman alderman.

23 Sir Henry Lytton started a farewell week performance in Gilbert and Sullivan at the Lyceum.

30 Prince Charles of Sweden paid a private visit to Sheffield.

May

1 Dr. L.H. Burrows celebrated twenty years as Bishop of Sheffield.

30 Brunswick Methodist Church celebrated its centenary.

June

16 An aeroplane crashed at Coal Aston taking part in a hospital pageant; nobody was injured.

18 Firth Brown Tools factory opened.

28 Oswald Mosley addressed a Fascist meeting at the City Hall.

Handsworth tram terminus at the Norfolk Hotel. The track was extended, and the terminus moved, to Orgreave Lane in 1934.

July

2 New employment exchange opened at West Street.

5 The Duchess of York opened the central Library and Graves Art Gallery.

11 Firth Brown and English Steel Corporation combined their stainless steel business in a new company called Firth Vickers Stainless Steels Ltd.

20 Tapton Court nurses' home opened.

22 Fairthorn Children's Convalescent Home opened.

August

7 Six men were injured in an explosion at Nunnery Colliery; two died later.

10 Alderman A.J. Blanchard resigned the leadership of Sheffield City Council Progressives group.

13 Mr Arthur Morley K.C. appointed Recorder of Sheffield.

21 Alderman Harold Jackson elected leader of the City Council Progressives group.

September

3   Mrs Burrows, wife of the Bishop of Sheffield, injured in an accident in Switzerland.

7   Handsworth tram service extended from Norfolk Hotel to Orgreave Lane.

26   Mr William Kean, of Sheffield, elected chairman of the TUC General Council.

27   Graves Trust announced the building of 100 houses to be let rent-free to aged Sheffield couples.

October

1   Work started on the restoration of Shrewsbury Chapel, Sheffield Cathedral.

2   Mr Alexander Williamson, general manager, United Steel Companies Ltd., installed Master Cutler.

3   Work started on building the Town Hall Square rock garden.

8   Richmond Sports Park (given by the Graves Trust) opened.

11   Sir Hilton Young, Minister of Health, opened the 2,000th house built by Sheffield Corporation for rehousing slum-dwellers.

18   Mr Walter Elliot, Minister for Agriculture, chief guest at the Cutlers' Feast.

November

9   Alderman P.J.M. Turner installed as Lord Mayor.

18   Firth Park tram service extended from Bellhouse Road to Sheffield Lane Top.

30   Announcement that Sheffield University needed £500,000 for extensions.

December

10   A nursery class started at Hammerton School, Attercliffe, the first nursery class in a Sheffield elementary school.

11   Bentley Bros. (Sheffield) Ltd.'s new garage and service centre opened in Savile Street with accommodation for one hundred cars.

13   Three men died after a roof fall at Birley East pit.

17   Sheffield Odd Job Week started, an effort to find pre-Christmas casual work for the unemployed.

18   Enlargement of St Paul's Church, Norton Lees, started.

Alderman J.G. Graves, the Sheffield businessman and benefactor, presented Tapton Court to the Royal Hospital for use as a nurses' home in 1933. It was opened in July 1934.

January

3   Mr Leslie Harcourt was appointed producer at Sheffield Repertory Theatre.

14   An airport would attract new industry to Sheffield, the Lord Mayor, Alderman P.J.M. Turner, told a Rotary Club dinner.

23   Inaugural meeting, Sheffield branch of the Women's Auxiliary of the YMCA.

February

6   Protest by 10,000 people in Town Hall Square over cuts in unemployment assistance ended in disorder; 23 people were arrested, several demonstrators and police were injured.

8   The unemployment assistance cuts were restored.

9   Colonel Sir Charles Clifford presented Broom Bank, Glossop Road, to Sheffield University for use as a dental hospital.

March

2   Sheffield's new telephone trunk exchange came into operation.

18   30mph speed limit in built-up areas came into force.

     An explosion in the electricity supplies blacked out The Wicker, Victoria Station and the Royal Victoria Hotel.

22   First compulsory driving tests in Sheffield.

26   Anonymous gifts of £50,000 and £23,000 made to the Royal Infirmary.

1935

28   Results of Sheffield Peace Ballot declared. Nearly 43 per cent of the electorate voted on six questions relating to world peace.

29   Graves Trust presented Tyzack's Dam and surrounding land at Beauchief to the city.

April

3   City Council refused to allow Sunday golf on municipal courses.

29   Sheffield Wednesday given a rousing welcome back to Sheffield after winning the FA Cup by beating West Bromwich Albion 4-2 (goals by Ellis Rimmer, 2, Palethorpe and Hooper). A crowd estimated at 100,000 gathered to see them bring the trophy back to Sheffield.

Mr Haydn Taylor, the man wrapped in the towel, being congratulated at Dover on August 22, 1935, after swimming the English Channel. It was the first time the channel had been swum that year.

Mr Taylor is one of Sheffield's less well known heroes. At the time the photograph was taken he was a dentist at Cleethorpes. But he was born in Sheffield, at the Palatine Buildings, Pinstone Street, went to Bow Street and Broomspring Lane schools, served in the City Battalion during the First World War, and was wounded in the Battle of the Somme on July 1, 1916. He started his swimming as a schoolboy in the city and in 1920 won the Sheffield, and the Yorkshire, 100 yards championships.

May

6   King George V's Silver Jubilee celebrations.

12   Oswald Mosley addressed a Fascist meeting at the City Hall.

15   George Lansbury MP addressed a Labour women's conference at the City Hall.

June

2   Sir Arthur Balfour elevated to the peerage as Baron Riverdale of Sheffield.

14   Mr J.A. Lyons, Prime Minister of Australia, visited Sheffield.

21 Alderman J.G. Graves gave 43 acres of land to add to Graves Park.

24 Mr G.W. Forbes, Prime Minister of New Zealand, visited Sheffield.

27 Archbishop of York at King Edward VII School speech day.

July

5 Mr Oliver Stanley, President of the Board of Education, was chief guest at the Forfeit Feast.

10 Great Yorkshire Show held at Coal Aston. The Prince of Wales visited the show on its second day.

31 Netherthorpe airfield opened.

August

7 A resolution to use Coal Aston as the site for a municipal airport was defeated in the City Council.

22 Mr Haydn Taylor, a dentist living in Cleethorpes but born in Sheffield, swam the English Channel.

September

29 A week-long celebration of the centenary of local government started.

30 Hartley Brook Road Council School opened.

October

2 City Council decided to prepare a scheme for building an aerodrome at Todwick, instead of Coal Aston.

8 Sir Samuel Roberts, MP for Ecclesall, installed as Master Cutler.

9 The Lord Chancellor, Viscount Hailsham, addressed an election meeting at the City Hall.

10 Lord Halifax, Secretary for War, is chief guest at the Cutlers' Feast.

14 Regal Cinema, Attercliffe, opened. It was previously the Royal Theatre.

November

9 Alderman Frank Thraves elected Lord Mayor.

14 General Election. Labour won Attercliffe, Brightside, Hillsborough and Park constituencies from the National Conservatives who kept their seats in Central, Ecclesall and Hallam.

25 Public appeal for funds for extensions to Sheffield University.

December

5 Berlin Philharmonic Orchestra, conducted by Wilhelm Furtwangler, played to a sell-out audience at the City Hall.

17 Eight back-to-back houses in Lord Street and Hague Lane were sold at auction for £12. Their leases had only nine months to run.

25 Hopes of a white Christmas were dashed. After a snowfall on Christmas Eve morning, Christmas Day was unusually mild.

On December 30, the Theatre Royal was destroyed by fire.

THEATRE

January

4 Woodseats and Beauchief Baptist Church, Hutcliffe Wood Road, opened.

15 Announcement that ten churches in the centre of Sheffield were to be demolished. The Ecclesiastical Commissioners subsequently approved the demolition of seven of the ten, but said the other three should remain.

20 King George V died. He was succeeded by King Edward VIII. The official proclamation of the new King was read by the Lord Mayor outside Sheffield Town Hall on January 22.

28 King George V's funeral. A crowd of 15,000 people gathered in Town Hall Square to pay tribute.

February

5 City Council decided to replace trams with buses on Fulwood via Broomhill route.

15 Carbrook Central Hall officially opened.

Whiteley Woods Hall was bought by Sheffield Girl Guides Association in 1936

March

4 St Katherine's Chapel, Sheffield Cathedral, consecrated and dedicated.

25 Church of the Sacred Heart, Hillsborough, opened.

April

2 Whiteley Woods Hall bought by Sheffield Girl Guides Association.

30 Sheffield Cathedral raised to its full status at a special service.

May

2 Sheffield Students' Union building, Leavygreave, opened.

13 Graves Trust decided to buy Ryegate, Manchester Road, to give to the Children's Hospital for use as a continuation hospital and convalescent home.

21 The enlarged Millhouses Methodist Church opened.

26 Clarke House opened as the new junior school of King Edward VII School.

June

2 Loxley Bros. Ltd., stationers, moved into their new shop at 57 Fargate.

1936

4 Alderman A.J. Bailey, chairman of the Transport Committee, said that one day a tunnel would be built from Moorhead to Castlegate to relieve city centre traffic.

11 The Hon. Bertram S.B. Stevens, Premier of New South Wales, visited Sheffield.

13 Hillsborough Golf Club's new pavilion opened.

July

5 Delegates to the International Congress on Glass, meeting in London, visited Sheffield for several days.

23 Launch of HMS Sheffield by the Duchess of Kent at Newcastle.

August

9 Sheffield athlete Ernest Harper won the silver medal in the Marathon at the Berlin Olympic Games.

19 In a referendum, five Sheffield council estates – Shiregreen, Manor, Wybourn, Arbourthorne and Woodthorpe – voted in favour of having public houses on the estates. Four other estates – Longley and Norwood, Stubbin and Brushes, Wisewood and High Wincobank – voted against.

23 Fulwood, via Broomhill, bus service started.

September

1 The Graves Trust opened its fiftieth old person's house, at Fairleigh, Manor.

HMS Sheffield – the Shiny Sheff – was launched by the Duchess of Kent at Newcastle in July 1936, and among the 10,000 people watching was a civic party from Sheffield. All its heavy forgings and stern frame castings were made in Sheffield, at English Steel Corporation Ltd.

2   The City Council decided that the stone lions on the stage of the City Hall should stay, even though the City Hall Committee had voted to remove them.

20   Bethel Chapel, Cambridge Street, closed.

29   Sheffield Corporation bought 70 acres of land near Whiteley Woods.

30   Woodthorpe Council School opened.

October

7   The City Council said it was 'not committed to building an aerodrome'.

Colonel W. Tozer, of Steel, Peech and Tozer Ltd., installed as Master Cutler.

14   Mr Anthony Eden, Foreign Secretary, was chief guest at the Cutlers' Feast.

15   New £10,000 swimming baths opened at King Edward VII School.

21   The Duke of Kent visited Sheffield, called at Painted Fabrics Ltd., Mappin and Webb's Queen's Road works, and the Napier Street works of James Neill and Co. Ltd. He also opened the extension to Tapton Court nurses' home and opened a Missions to Seamen exhibition.

November

2   Municipal elections; the Progressives gained one seat from Labour.

4   It was announced that the Home Secretary had approved an Assize Court for Sheffield in 1940.

9   Sheffield elected its first woman Lord Mayor, Cllr. Mrs A.E. Longden.

December

2   Mr A.R. Fearnley retired as manager of Sheffield Transport Department.

10   Abdication of King Edward VIII

14   A large crowd gathered outside Sheffield Town Hall to hear King George VI proclaimed.

29   The ornamental garden in Barkers Pool was presented to the city by Alderman J.G. Graves.

Sheffield's first woman Lord Mayor, Cllr. Mrs Ann Eliza Longden, was elected in 1936. During her year of office she was also the first woman ever to attend a Cutlers' Feast. She is seen here leading the Civic Sunday procession a few days after her election.

January

10   The old colours of the 1st Battalion Coldstream Guards were laid up in Sheffield Cathedral.

February

25   The Archbishop of Canterbury, Dr. Cosmo Gordon Lang, dedicated the Episcopal Throne at Sheffield Cathedral in memory of the Rt. Revd. John Nathaniel Quirk, who was Bishop Suffragen of Sheffield from 1901 to 1914. Among those in the congregation were the Princess Royal and her husband, the Earl of Harewood.

The Archbishop also opened Crewe Hall, Sheffield University's new hall of residence.

March

23   Exhibition of Air Raid Precautions at the Central Ambulance Station.

29   More than 30,000 people watched the annual Darnall Medical Aid Society parade.

April

14   Ryegate, the new annexe of the Children's Hospital, was formally opened.

16   The rebuilt and enlarged Weston Park Museum was formally opened by Sir Philip Sassoon, Under Secretary of State for Air.

19   Sheffield Musical Society decided to amalgamate with Sheffield Philharmonic Society.

27   Nearly 300 acres of land at Fulwood and Whirlow were presented to the city by the Graves Trust.

May

1   Sheffield Wednesday lost 1-0 to Huddersfield Town at Huddersfield in their last match of the season and were relegated to the Second Division. (Sheffield United were already in the second).

12   King George VI was crowned at Westminster Abbey. A Royal Salute of 31 guns was fired in Norfolk Park, streets and buildings were decorated and 700 troops paraded through Sheffield city centre. The Corporation entertained 10,000 old people to tea. In the evening, the band and drums of the Hallamshires beat the retreat in Barkers Pool, and bonfires were lit all over the city. Fireworks displays had to be postponed because of the rain. Celebrations went on for a week.

June

10   Thousands of schoolchildren presented a Coronation Year Historical Pageant at Bramall Lane.

21   Frecheville Community Centre officially opened by Sir Enoch Hill, president of the Halifax Building Society.

29   Sir Thomas Inskip, Minister for Co-ordination of Defence, was chief guest at the Forfeit feast.

July

3   Plans announced for Sheffield's Civic Centre, including new law courts and police HQ in Arundel Street, a new College of Arts and Crafts, also in Arundel Street, Town Hall extensions, and plans to widen Arundel Street, Surrey Street and Norfolk Street to 60 feet.

14   The Albert Hall, Barkers Pool, was destroyed by fire.

31   Herbert Sutcliffe scored his 100th century for Yorkshire against Lancashire at Bramall Lane.

Yorkshire cricket doesn't arouse quite the same passions these days, but the name of this man, Herbert Sutcliffe, photographed here on the old practice area at Bramall Lane, is still revered throughout the county. The young lad with him is his son, Billy, who grew up to play for, and captain, the county team.

Partnering Jack Hobbs for England, or Percy Holmes for Yorkshire, Herbert Sutcliffe became a legendary figure in cricket. 'He is great,' said R.C. Robertson-Glasgow, the cricket writer. 'Great in idea, and great in effect'. He scored more than 50,000 runs in 21 years, more than 2,700 of them for England against Australia, at an average of nearly 67 an innings, and he made more than 100 centuries for Yorkshire. They could do with him today.

He scored his 100th century for Yorkshire at Bramall Lane in a match against Lancashire on July 31 1937, the traditional Bank Holiday fixture, and the Sheffield crowd gave him an ovation never seen at the ground before. 'Crowd's homage to a great player,' said the *Sheffield Telegraph*, over a match report in which the paper's cricket writer described it as 'a remarkable demonstration of admiration, congratulation and affection'.

1937

Sheffield members of the 49 West Riding Division (T.A.) Royal Engineers spent a fortnight near Scarborough, on their annual camp in August 1937. They practised building bridges, blowing up bridges, and (as pictured) digging clifftop trenches. According to a contemporary report, their food consumption doubled within days.

August

4   City Council approved buying the site of St Paul's Church and churchyard.

11   First road and rail enquiry bureau in the country opened near the Midland Station.

September

27   The LMS Railway speeded up its Sheffield to London service cutting half-an-hour off the three and a half hour journey.

October

4   Batchelor's Peas Ltd.'s new canning factory at Wadsley Bridge, the largest in England, formally opened.

7   Colonel F.A. Neill, chairman and managing director of James Neill and Co. (Sheffield) Ltd., installed as Master Cutler.

15   The Lord Mayor, Cllr. Mrs A.E. Longden, and a civic party visited *HMS Sheffield at Immingham. Next day officers and men from the ship visited Sheffield. The Lord Mayor gave a dance for them and they saw the Sheffield Wednesday - Sheffield United match at Hillsborough.*

21   *King George VI and Queen Elizabeth visited Sheffield for one and a half hours as part of a three-day tour of Yorkshire, and made an appearance on the Town Hall balcony.*

November

1   *The Lord Mayor, Cllr. Mrs A.E. Longden, became the first woman to attend a Cutlers' Feast. Dr. E.L. Burgin, Minister of Transport was chief guest.*

Municipal elections: no change on the City Council.

7   *Mr Billy Walker resigned as secretary-manager of Sheffield Wednesday.*

9   *Alderman E.G. Rowlinson elected Lord Mayor of Sheffield.*

17   *Governors of the Royal Hospital (on West Street) and the Royal Infirmary (on Infirmary Road) agreed that the two hospitals should amalgamate.*

December

6   *Ritz Cinema, Parson Cross, opened.*

12   *Last services held in St. Paul's Church, Pinstone Street, before its demolition.*

27   *Plaza Cinema, Handsworth, opened.*

A handwritten note on the back of this photograph says that it shows Millhouses Park. It might be. But I suspect it is more likely to be Abbeydale Park, where a large charity gala was held most years around August Bank Holiday. A wire walker called Rococo appeared at the Abbeydale Park gala on at least one occasion, in 1937. It could be him.

1938

January

19 St John Fisher Roman Catholic Church, Bawtry Road, opened the first church in the diocese to be dedicated to a Yorkshire Cardinal.

Woodthorpe Council School swimming baths opened, the first to be built at a Sheffield elementary school.

23 St Timothy's Church, Crookes, damaged by fire.

31 Arbourthorne Central Council School opened.

February

2 The City Council approved the replanning of central Sheffield, with new roads and the creation of residential and industrial zones.

18 Adolf Busch and Rudolf Serkin refused to start a recital at the City Memorial Hall because of noise from the ballroom. After negotiations, the dance band agreed to take out several wind instruments, and the recital started half an hour late.

22 Bertrand Russell told a meeting at the Central Library that nothing of real human value could be preserved by fighting. Pacifism was the only way to peace.

March

19 Memorial plaque to Sir Charles Clegg unveiled in the Sheffield Wednesday boardroom.

26 Sheffield's Youth Hostel, Ravenstor, Miller's Dale, officially opened.

April

1 Lady Riverdale presented Sheffield Sea Cadets with their colours.

7 Fire caused £50,000 damage at George Bassett and Co. Ltd., Owlerton.

8 Conductor Sir Thomas Beecham made one of his regular criticisms of the stone lions on the City Hall stage – 'strange specimens of natural history'.

May

7 Consecration of St Hilda's Church, Shiregreen.

12 Beck Road Council School, Shiregreen, opened.

31 Mr. Winston Churchill told a City Hall meeting that Britain's re-armament programme should be speeded up.

June

28 Firth Park Maternity and Child Welfare Centre opened.

Coisley Hill Sewage Works opened.

29 The Duke of Kent inaugurated a new gasholder at Sheffield Gas Company's Low Wincobank works, visited Atlas and Norfolk Works and Vickers Works.

July

19 The Duchess of Gloucester inaugurated Sheffield Voluntary Hospitals' Million Pounds Appeal, opened a new ward at the Children's Hospital, and laid the foundation stone of a new maternity block at the Jessop Hospital for Women.

When the Duke of Kent inaugurated a new gas holder at Lower Wincobank in June 1938, a contingent of 62 ex-servicemen, all employees of the gas company, formed a guard of honour. The Duke also met four veteran employees, all over 65, including a man of 78 who had worked for the company for more than 63 years.

August

Sheffield experienced its first black-out for testing air raid precautions.

5   Carlton Cinema opened.

?2 Prof. J.L. Wheatley, former Director of the National Gallery of South Africa, was appointed Director of Art Galleries in Sheffield, succeeding Dr. J.K.M. Rothenstein, who was appointed Director of the Tate Gallery.

24 Sheffield Corporation bought the Albert Hall site in Barkers Pool for £50,000.

27 Zachary Merton Convalescent Home, Fulwood, opened.

September

3   Longley Park open air swimming pool, paid for by Mr G.H. Lawrence, opened.

17 Forum Cinema, Southey, opened.

26 The Graves Trust presented Forge Dam, Fulwood, and Old May House Farm, Mayfield Valley, to the city.

War crisis brought on by tension between Germany and Czechoslovakia. Gas masks were issued in Sheffield, trenches dug in parks and recreation grounds, and anti-aircraft guns were mounted at various points.

October

4   Mr A.J. Grant, managing director of Thos. Firth and John Brown Ltd., installed as Master Cutler.

10 Film star Tom Mix appeared at the Empire with his wonder horse, Tony.

22 Sheffield had its second blackout. RAF planes flew over to check how much of the city's heavy industry might be seen by enemy bombers.

24 The Sheffield Telegraph appeared with news, instead of advertisements, on its front page for the first time.

31 The Daily Independent was amalgamated with the Sheffield Telegraph.

November

1   Municipal elections. The Progressives gained one seat.

3   Sheffield United signed Jimmy Hagan from Derby County for £2,925.

9   Alderman W.J. Hunter installed as Lord Mayor.

14 Sir Kingsley Wood, Secretary of State for Air, addressed a City Hall meeting.

December

2   Arthur Bliss conducted one of his own works, the suite from the ballet Checkmate, at the City Hall.

6   Dr. Arthur W. Barton, chief physics master, Repton School, appointed headmaster of King Edward VII School, Sheffield.

8   Film star Jessie Matthews opened The Star Doll Show at the Cutlers' Hall.

14 Revd. William Wallace chosen as new superintendent of Sheffield Methodist Mission.

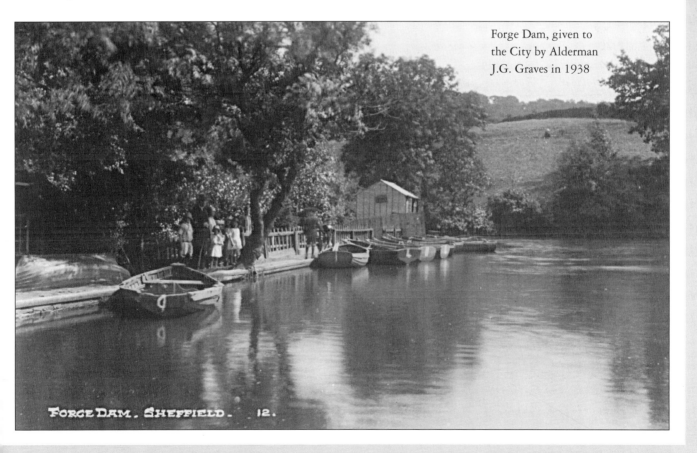

Forge Dam, given to the City by Alderman J.G. Graves in 1938

FORGE DAM. SHEFFIELD.   12.

Dr. Leonard Hedley Burrows, Bishop of Sheffield, expressed sorrow in January 1939 that Sheffield had not cared better for its antiquities. It was sad, he said, that probably the oldest inhabited house in the city was the one he lived in, Bishopsholme, at Norwood.

Dr. Burrows would have been even sadder if he had known the eventual fate of Bishopsholme, seen here in a winter setting in 1939. The new Bishop, consecrated later in the year, moved to another house, the Corporation bought Bishopsholme in 1940, and it reverted to its old name, Norwood Hall. After years of neglect, vandalism and controversy, it was demolished in 1976.

January

5   *Fire badly damaged the Randall Street cutlery works of R.F. Mosley and Co. Ltd.*

12   *St Oswald's church hall, Millhouses, opened.*

13   *Film star Anna Neagle visited the Central Picture House, The Moor, where her film Sixty Glorious Years was being shown.*

February

10   *Arbourthorne Hotel opened, the first public house built on a Sheffield council estate.*

14   *The Princess Royal attended the hallowing of Sheffield Cathedral extensions.*

22   *Sheffield United bought international outside-left Bobby Reid from Brentford for £6000, record fee for a Sheffield club.*

March

10   *Sheffield United sold centre-forward Ephraim (Jock) Dodds to Blackpool for £10,000, a record fee for both clubs.*

25   *St Cecilia's Church, Parson Cross, consecrated.*

April

1   *Darnall Wesley Methodist church opened.*

15   *Mount Tabor Methodist Church, Parson Cross, opened.*

16   *Pensioners marched through Sheffield to a mass meeting at Burngreave demanding higher pensions.*

May

1   *New operating theatre block opened at the Royal Infirmary.*

6   *Sheffield United promoted to the First Division (after five years in the Second). By beating Tottenham Hotspur 6-1 in the last match of the season they pushed Sheffield Wednesday into third place.*

10   *Mr Roland Jennings won Hallam constituency for the Conservatives in a by-election caused by the death of Sir Louis Smith.*

22   *Jazz pianist Fats Waller and the Mills Brothers appeared at the Empire for a week.*

June

6   *The Freedom of Sheffield was conferred on the Bishop, Dr. L.H. Burrows, Sir Robert Hadfield and Mr Harry Brearley.*

12   *Headquarters of Sheffield University Department of Glass Technology opened.*

The chap in the top hat is Jan Van Albert, a Dutchman said to be 9 foot 3½ inches tall. The little chap at his side is his brother-in-law, Seppetoni, a Swiss midget. They appeared together at the *Sheffield Empire* in May 1939 in a show called *Would You Believe It?* Also on the bill were Elroy, a man with no arms who played the trumpet with his feet, a pig that jumped hurdles, a man who wrestled with a lioness and a xylophone player who used a skull instead of a xylophone.

It was one surprise after another, as one reviewer said.

Sheffield was on the verge of getting its own Assize Court in 1939 and by way of preparation the Corporation bought Parkhead House, Ecclesall Road South, former home of Sir Robert Hadfield, to use as Judges' Lodgings. Four months later, the Second World War started and Sheffield's hopes of becoming an Assize Town were dashed. It was not until 1955 that the Assizes were set up and by then another house, at Whirlow, had been chosen as Judges' Lodgings.

July

1   *Sir John Simon, Chancellor of the Exchequer, made honorary Doctor of Laws at Sheffield University.*

13   *Farewell presentations to the Bishop, Dr. L.H. Burrows, at a City Hall meeting.*

20   *Weston Park weather centre recorded .77 inches of rain in twenty minutes during a heavy thunderstorm. There was widespread flooding and lightning struck several houses.*

21   *New assembly hall opened by the Dowager Duchess of Norfolk at the Royal Sheffield Institution for the Blind.*

24   *Rex cinema, Intake, opened.*

August

2   *The City Council approved revised plans for a bus station at Pond Street.*

21   *Air raid siren tests carried out at all English Steel Corporation's Sheffield works.*

30   *All 20,000 lights in Sheffield side streets were blacked out all night as a precaution against air raids.*

September

2   *About 9000 children, disabled and blind people and expectant mothers were evacuated from Sheffield because of the imminence of war.*

3   *Great Britain declared war on Germany. Blackout orders came into force. All street lighting was switched off, all schools, cinemas and theatres closed.*

15   *Theatres and cinemas were allowed to re-open.*

18   *Capitol cinema, Sheffield Lane Top, opened.*

22   *Petrol rationing started.*

October

3   *Mr Ashley Skelton Ward, joint managing director of Thos. W. Ward Ltd., installed as Master Cutler.*

14   *Enthronement of the Rt. Revd. Leslie S. Hunter as Bishop of Sheffield. He had been consecrated at York Minster on September 29.*

November

1   *Municipal elections were cancelled.*

     The first of half-a-million ration books were sent out in Sheffield.

9   *Alderman John Arthur Longden installed as Lord Mayor.*

20   *Sheffield had its first genuine air raid warning, but there was no air raid.*

25   *Golfer Henry Cotton played at Abbeydale in aid of the British Red Cross.*

December

2   *Consecration of St Paul's Church, Arbourthorne.*

10   *Sheffield's thirty-six air raid sirens were tested.*

15   *The Fleur de Lys public house, Fargate, opened as a forces' social centre.*

1939

C.535.   KING STREET, SHEFFIELD. (13)

KING STREET (*above*) in 1935, showing the rear of C & A on the right. Five years later nearly every building on the street was destroyed in the blitz. The shop facing up the street is the old Woolworths 3*d.* and 6*d.* store, with its 'cafeteria seating 400'. You don't see cafeterias these days.

Angel Street and Snig Hill are seen on a sunny day in the early 1930s (*right*). Most of the buildings shown were destroyed in the 1940 blitz, among them Cockayne's and the old *Angel Hotel* on the left, Syminton and Croft's shop, F. G. Thomas, stationers, and King's Chambers on the right. Among the men, flat caps and bowlers are much in evidence, and all the women wear cloche hats and fur collars – except one older woman who is wearing a shawl.

TWO 1936 VIEWS of Button Lane, off Moorhead, looking towards the *Nelson Hotel* and the Public Benefit Boot Co. Ltd. Button Lane has been completely obliterated by modern redevelopment. It was roughly where Debenhams is today. As the picture *(above)* was taken a lady in the middle distance was bending down tending her dog. She had probably spotted the other dog, left, and was taking action to avoid any chance of bother between the two. The only other notable feature is the fine selection of wall lamps on the buildings to the left.

The second picture *(left)* is taken looking the other way, by a photographer standing roughly where the delivery van is on the first picture.

St Paul's Church, Pinstone Street – seen here from Moorhead – closed on 12 December, 1937. The building was demolished and there was talk of a cinema, shops or offices being built on the site.

Another idea, put forward by two local civil engineers, was for an 80-foot deep, oval, reinforced concrete, bomb-proof car park, with five subterranean levels that would have room for 400 cars in peacetime, or 10,000 people in an air raid. The idea was not taken up. Instead, the site became gardens.

When the old church was demolished the bells were preserved and moved to a new church, also called St Paul's, at Arbourthorne.

BY OCTOBER 1938, the site of St. Paul's Church had been levelled though the former church boundary walls and railings were still in place. When the new layout was finished it was officially known as St Paul's Gardens, after the old church. The people of Sheffield largely ignored this name and called them the Peace Gardens. Half a century later the City Council decided there was not much point continuing with an official name that most people ignored and made the Peace Gardens their official name.

The Town Hall has a two-tone appearance here. The darker portion is the original building, and the lighter portion is part of the extensions opened by the Prince of Wales in 1923. Since then there has been another, less elegant extension.

MILK BARS were a 1930s phenomenon. They specialised in frothy milk shakes and Horlicks drinks, both prepared on a kind of mechanical agitator attached to the bar. The constituents were poured into a metal jug, the jug was clipped to the agitator, and the agitator was switched on. The noise it made as it mixed the drink and created the froth was half gurgle, half whirr, a sound unique to milk bars.

The other surviving memory for most people is the smell of the milk shakes, a slightly sweet, milky, strawberry-ish smell that could be quite tempting.

Marsden's had two milk bars in Sheffield, the better known probably the one on Pinstone Street, opposite the Peace Gardens. Jack Payne, the famous bandleader *(left),* is seen operating the agitator after he had performed the official opening of one of them.

The lower picture shows members of staff standing by their agitators, ready for action. The notice behind them advertises Ice Cream Sodas at 6*d.*, Sundæs at 8*d.*, Melbas and Banana Splits at one shilling, Cream Ices at 4*d.* and 6*d.* and coffee at 4*d.* For decimalised modern drinkers, this means there was nothing over 5p (one shilling).

Marsden's are still very much in business, of course, but milk bars went out of fashion a long time ago.

THE LOCATION is Station Road, Darnall, but I don't know exactly when, or what the occasion was. An obvious guess is that it was the parish church segment of the annual Darnall Medical Aid Parade which always attracted large crowds, especially if the weather was half decent.

FOR ALL THE SAINTS

R.I.P.

I HAVEN'T THE faintest idea where or when the photograph above was taken. Its caption has gone missing. My guess is that it was taken during one of the 1930s royal event celebrations; either the Jubilee celebrations of King George V in 1935, or the Coronation celebrations of King George VI in 1937. There were street parties, bunting and Union Flags all over Sheffield on both occasions.

Even without the precise details, it seemed too good to leave out. On past experience, somebody will be able to tell me where and when it was taken.

It still happens every year (*left*): people from all over the city dress up in whatever takes their fancy and tramp round the streets in the Star Walk, some because they are competitive walkers, some to raise money for charity, some for a bet, and some for no special reason, except that it seemed like a good idea at the time they decided to do it.

This is the 1935 walk, on its way down High Street. Two of the walkers, number 23 and the chap behind him, are wearing strong black boots, one of the others seems to have his everyday shoes on, but most have plumped for plimsolls or tennis pumps. Trainers, as worn for 1990s Star walking – and just about everything else – had not been invented in 1935.

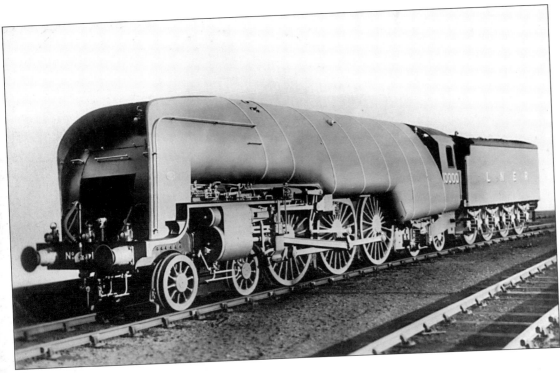

THE SO-CALLED 'hush-hush' locomotive, Sir Nigel Gresley's odd-looking 4-6-4 number 10000, went on display at Sheffield Victoria Station in May 1932. The engine was not an enormous success and it was later rebuilt to look like one of Gresley's streamlined Pacifics, although it kept its 4-6-4 wheel arrangement.

Buses replaced tramcars on the Nether Edge route on March 25, 1934, the first major route to be converted. Elsewhere in the city trams ruled supreme throughout the decade. This bunch was photographed at Queen's Road depot in 1938.

THE FULWOOD via Broomhill tram route along Fulwood Road [cl]osed in August 1936. Not [en]ough people used it. The car [h]eading back towards town [al]ong Fulwood Road (*above*), on [t]his picture seems to prove the [p]oint. It looks as though there's [o]nly one passenger sitting on [t]he top deck.

The tramcar to the right [a]ppeared in several guises [b]etween 1937 and 1939. It [t]oured the streets in 1937 with [t]he words 'Coronation' and 'Long May They Reign' on its [s]ides to mark the Coronation of King George VI. It was [m]odified and illuminated in October the same year, when [t]he King and Queen Elizabeth [v]isited Sheffield, and the wording was changed to 'Welcome to Our King and Queen'. A year later the soldiers

in the alcoves were changed to policemen and the wording was changed to 'Safety First' for a special road safety campaign. And in 1939, the policemen vacated the alcoves and were

replaced by nurses, fireman and suchlike, and the wording was changed to 'Serve to Save, Sheffield is Not Ready' as part of an A.R.P. recruitment campaign.

A different design – but possibly the same tram – was used for the Jubilee of King George V and the holding of the Great Yorkshire Show in Sheffield, in 1935.

THE J.D. COOK and Beard Homes, Kent Road, Meersbrook (*below*), was a block of eight houses for old couples, paid for by Mrs J. J. Beard in memory of her brother, Mr J.D. Cook, local benefactor and former councillor for the Heeley ward. It was opened in May 1935.

Wilson Road Synagogue (*right*) was opened in April 1930.

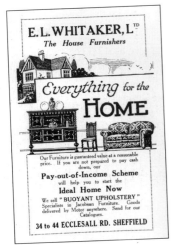

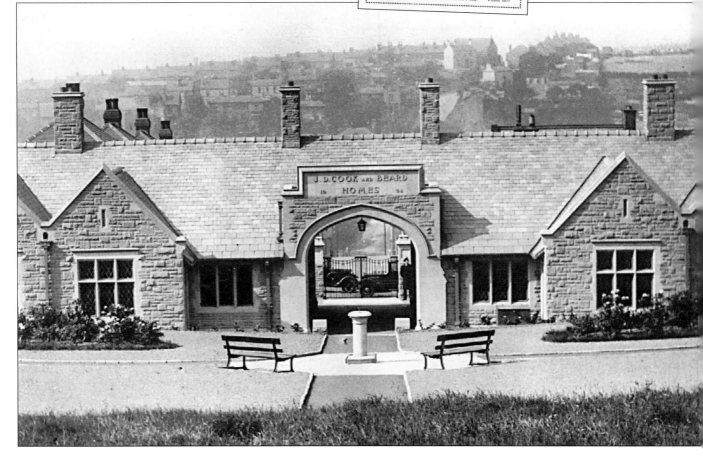

T HE NEW Employment
Exchange, West Street,
seen *(right)*, nearing
completion in 1934.

The idea behind the Ministry
of Labour Overseas Settlement
Office at 165 Norfolk Street,
(below), (next to Hatfield's
Garage) was to help local people,
especially those who were
unemployed, to find work in
other countries.

FAIRTHORN Children's Convalescent Home *(above)* opened in 1934. The Church of the Sacred Heart, Hillsborough, opened two years later, in 1936.

THE THIRD WEEK of June, 1939, was a good week for the drinking fraternity in Sheffield. Tennant Brothers Ltd. opened three large new public houses within two days: the *Parson Cross Hotel*, seen above nearing completion, the *Sicey Hotel*, Shiregreen, and the *Highcliffe Hotel*, Greystones.

SHEFFIELD Central
Conservative Association's
new headquarters in
Wilkinson Street were opened
in January 1939. At first the
building was called Neville
House, after Prime Minister
Neville Chamberlain. The name
was dropped later after
Chamberlain lost favour.
Batchelors' Peas Ltd.'s new
canning factory at Wadsley
Bridge *(below)*, the largest in
England, was opened in 1937.

ANYBODY who doesn't remember the old Walker and Hall works at the corner of Eyre Street and Howard Street, *(below)*, might think that those were real flags fluttering atop the building. They were not. They were made of metal so they looked exactly like this even on a day when there wasn't the slightest bit of wind blowing. As a child they fascinated me every time I saw them. They were not just a gimmick, though. The W & H flag was the firm's trademark. Eyre Street is the street going off to the right, and the pictur was taken in May 1934.

A suggestion was made in 1938 that Ponds Forge *(left)*, one of the oldest works in the city, should be moved to another site to help the Corporation's town planning ideas. 'Absurd,' said one of the directors of George Senior and Sons Ltd., the owners. The forg was near the railway and the canal. It couldn't just be moved. And it wasn't.

ETHER CUT WHEEL
(*above*), was one of
the last wheels to
work on the Rivelin. It closed
as a scythe grinding wheel in
the mid-1930s. The dam was
preserved, but the buildings
were demolished.

The Grogram Wheel (*left*),
sometimes locally called the
Groggie, was also on the
Rivelin. It went out of use
about 1933. Hardly anything is
left of it today. In the 1930s
there were still the remains of
more than twenty wheels in the
Rivelin Valley. Most of the
machinery was removed for
scrap in the early years of the
Second World War, and the
buildings were either
vandalised or demolished.

The *TELEGRAPH* and *Star* offices by night. Two of the shops on ▢ frontage were the Sheffield G▢ Company showrooms and the ▢ one next door was occupied b▢ Bell and Co.'s blouse shop.

Sheffield's two morning newspapers, the *Telegraph* (founded 1855) and the *Independent* (founded 1819) amalgamated in 1938. There must have been some very surprised and puzzled newspaper buyers in the city ▢ the morning of October 31 when, without any advance notice, the two papers came o▢ as one. In later years the *Independent* half of the title shrank, and eventually disappeared altogether.

FUN
FOR
ALL

Children of all ages will enjoy the Pictures and Stories in this Comic Annual about the Queer Adventures of Gloops, the world's funniest Cat.

GLOOPS
BIRTHDAY NUMBER

NOW ON SALE – PRICE 2D.

The Sheffield University.

S HEFFIELD UNIVERSITY was still a relatively small place, but it had started to expand. During the 1930s, Broom Bank, Glossop Road was presented to the university as a dental hospital, the Students' Union, Leavygreave, and the headquarters of the Department of Glass Technology opened, and a new hall of residence, Crewe Hall *(right)*, opened in February 1937.

POND STREET changed beyond all recognition in the late 1930s following the City Council's decision to clear the area and build a large central bus station.

The brewery of Thomas Rawson and Co. Ltd., pictured (left) in 1938, stood roughly where part of Sheffield Hallam University stands today. Beyond the brewery, going towards Fitzalan Square, the street was narrow, with only just enough room for tram tracks, and hemmed in by drab, three-storey houses and shops. The projecting part of the brewery, shown on the first picture, can be seen (below) on the right hand side.

Two of the Pond Street shops that were cleared were George Binns, gents' hairdresser, and Mary Brown's dining rooms, (right). The hairdresser's was said to have been built over the famous Ponds Well, once widely known for its alleged medicinal qualities.

The brewery and the old houses were no great loss, but there was some concern that the 14th century Hall in the Ponds building, nearby, Sheffield's only remaining timbered building (right), might also be lost in the clearance. Members of the Hunter Archaeological Society, keen to see it preserved, suggested that it could become a refreshment house for the new bus station. It was preserved, as the Queen's Head Hotel.

43

IN THE PLANNING stages Sheffield City Council referred to the new street in the photograph above as River Don Street, but at the last minute changed its mind and chose the name Castlegate instead. It was a wise decision.

The picture was taken as work neared completion, a few days before the street was officially opened to traffic on November 23, 1930. One driver seems to have jumped the gun.

To make way for Castlegate to be built, the building next to Lady's Bridge (*left*) had been demolished. The shop on the corner was having a clearance sale as the picture was taken, getting ready to move out.

THE PICTURE to the right looks like a puzzle picture, but it isn't. This is a bird's-eye view of Town Hall Square, with Leopold Street tram track at the top, Fargate off to the right, and Pinstone Street out of sight to the left. At least, it's the view the birds' eyes used to have before upper parts of the Town Hall were cocooned in netting to stop them roosting on its sills and ledges.

The picture was taken from the Town Hall tower to show how a one-way traffic system was supposed to work. Faced with increasing traffic problems, the Corporation tried a number of schemes in this area in the 1930s.

To give more road space, the old statue of Queen Victoria was moved to Endcliffe Park in February 1930. The place where it stood can be seen from the large circle on the road surface. Four months later, traffic for The Moor was diverted along Surrey Street, Norfolk Street and Union Street and only tram cars were allowed to go direct from Fargate to Moorhead.

The next change, in 1931, involved a policeman controlling traffic from a rather odd podium, bottom right on the picture. It quickly became known to locals as the ice cream kiosk and it remained an entertaining diversion for everybody until September 1933, when two-way traffic was resumed on Pinstone Street.

In 1934, the junction was re-arranged yet again. A rock garden was built, with pedestrian crossings lined in white, one of which followed a path through the rock garden, as the lower picture shows

TOWN HALL SQUARE, SHEFFIELD

N O PROBLEMS with double yellow lines, parking meters or traffic wardens in the 1930s. You could swan down to Paradise Square, leave your Austin Seven or your Wolsley Nine on the cobbles and nip off for a spot of shopping without fear of being booked, clamped or prosecuted. One of the ladies in the picture seem to be having trouble of a different kind, persuading her little dog that it should go with her.

The irony behind the picture of Leader House, Surrey Street (left), is that it was taken in June 1937 when the building was under threat of demolition to make way for a new School of Art. As things turned out, the Art School went elsewhere, just about every other building on the picture was demolished, or destroyed by bombing, and Leader House is still there in the 1990s.

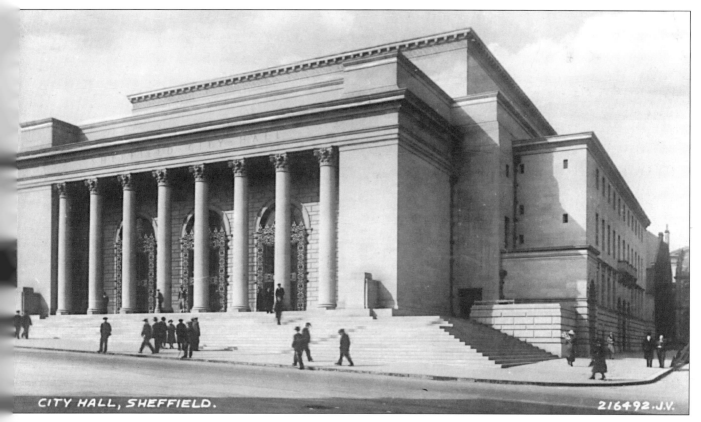

CITY HALL, SHEFFIELD.

216492.J.V.

THE POOR OLD City Hall has been in a mess all its life. Even before [it] opened, on 22 September [1]932, it was the cause of [c]ontroversy. There were long [a]rguments about what it should [b]e called. Some people wanted [i]t to be called the Memorial [H]all, as a tribute to Sheffield's [w]ar dead. A large petition was [s]ubmitted. The City Council [p]referred to call it the City [H]all, but after a lot of argey-[b]argey, arrived at a [c]ompromise. The building [w]ould be the City Hall, the [l]arge hall inside it would be the [O]val Hall, and the smaller hall [a]t the rear of the building [w]ould be the City (Memorial) [H]all.

There was another controversy about its cost, £364,000, which was £80,000 more than the original estimate.

There was an even more complicated argument about a proposed inscription around a frieze in the Oval Hall. The City Council decided on a quotation from Ruskin, then

found it was too long to fit on the frieze. Other quotations were suggested and the whole business eventually became so involved that the council decided not to have an inscription at all.

Within days of the opening another row started. A letter

writer to the *Sheffield Daily Telegraph* said the Assyrian stone lions on the stage of the Oval Hall were out of keeping with the rest of the interior and ought to be scrapped. Other people agreed, and the City Hall Committee decided to get rid of the lions. The City

Council overturned this and said the lions must stay. And stay they did, for another 30 years, during which they were the target of intermittent sniping sarcasm from famous orchestral conductors, visiting musicians and several generations of concertgoers.

The Choir Stalls, and Organ, Sheffield City Hall. 6298.

O F ALL THE STREETS in central Sheffield, Church Street (above) has probably altered least. The tramcars have gone, the shop tenants have changed, and the shop fronts have been modernised. But overall, the street looks remarkably similar in the 1990s to what it was in August 1932 when this picture was taken. Even the building of the Orchard Square development has not made much difference.

Considering the number of bombs that dropped around him in December 1940, the number of nearby buildings that caught fire or were demolished, the number of times Fitzalan Square (left) has been remodelled, and Sheffield's unfortunate habit of getting fed up with its monuments and carting them off to early retirement in a suburban park, King Edward VII has done remarkably well to stay put since this picture was taken in April 1938.

Even on High Street (opposite) there was a relaxed attitude to parking, although parked cars and trams, between them, reduced the traffic flow in places to a narrow single line.

One oddity shown on the High Street picture is the old traffic sign on the street light at the junction of Fargate and Church Street. It points up Fargate, which, it says, is the route to London, Baslow, Bakewell and Hathersage – a somewhat random selection of destinations.

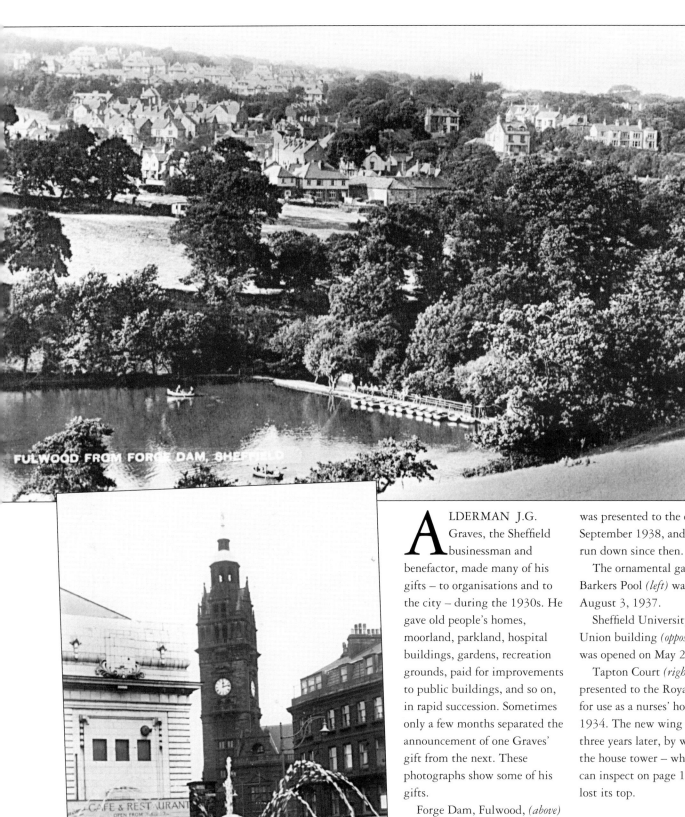

FULWOOD FROM FORGE DAM, SHEFFIELD

ALDERMAN J.G. Graves, the Sheffield businessman and benefactor, made many of his gifts – to organisations and to the city – during the 1930s. He gave old people's homes, moorland, parkland, hospital buildings, gardens, recreation grounds, paid for improvements to public buildings, and so on, in rapid succession. Sometimes only a few months separated the announcement of one Graves' gift from the next. These photographs show some of his gifts.

Forge Dam, Fulwood, (*above*)

was presented to the city in September 1938, and has sadly run down since then.

The ornamental garden in Barkers Pool (*left*) was opened August 3, 1937.

Sheffield University Students Union building (*opposite, top*) was opened on May 2, 1936.

Tapton Court (*right*) was presented to the Royal Hospital for use as a nurses' home in 1934. The new wing was built three years later, by which time the house tower – which you can inspect on page 15 – had lost its top.

WITHIN the space of a little over eighteen months Sheffield lost two of its best-known city-centre buildings in fires. The *Theatre Royal* (*this page*), at the corner of Arundel Street and Tudor Street, burned down on December 30, 1935; and the *Albert Hall*, Barkers Pool (*opposite*), was destroyed on July 14, 1937. Neither of them was rebuilt.

The *Theatre Royal* was one of the oldest theatres in the provinces, first built 1773, and rebuilt in the 1850s. Although firemen were on the scene quickly, within an hour only the outer walls remained. At the height of the blaze precautions were taken to stop the fire spreading to the nearby *Lyceum Theatre*, the Central Library and the Adelphi Hotel. The cause of the fire was not known. The theatre had not been in use for 28 hours before it started.

The following morning, the top photograph was taken from the roof of the Central Library building. And six months later, (*below*) the last section of the remains was being demolished. The site is now an open area in front of the *Lyceum*.

THE *ALBERT HALL*
opened in 1873 for
music, entertainment
and public meetings. It had one
of the finest concert organs in
the country. Many famous
politicians and public figures
spoke there. It, too, burned
quickly, and the best firemen
could do was prevent the fire
spreading to neighbouring
buildings.

The *Albert Hall* was burned
down on the night of July 14,
1937. Firemen were
photographed working on the
Burgess Street side of the hall
during the blaze.

On the following morning,
crowds gathered in Barkers Pool
to see the damage.

CARR BRIDGE PATH,
Porter Brook, in April
1931, shortly after the

Corporation had built paths and
opened the area to the public.

SOME VERY famous people have passed through the gates of Concord Park, (*right*), among them Horatio Nelson, the Duke of Cumberland (uncle to King George III), and William Pitt, the first Earl of Chatham, who once owned them. The wrought iron gates were originally at the entrance to a large house called Hayes Park Place, Kent, which was built and lived in by William Pitt. In later years it was the home of Sir Everard Hambro. In 1932 the house was pulled down, and Mr Charles Boot, head of the Sheffield firm Henry Boot and Sons Ltd., who carried out the work, ensured that worthwhile relics from the house were preserved. Among them were the gates, which Mr Boot presented to the City Council for use at Concord Park.

In his letter to the Town Clerk, Mr Boot quoted Pitt's speech after the Battle of Trafalgar in which he said: 'Let us hope that England, having saved herself by her energy, may save Europe by her example.'

Mr Boot added: 'May the gates still open to some who will carry Pitt's message; it may well be true again today.'

The park was a gift of Alderman J.G. Graves, the famous benefactor. He chose the name Concord as a reflection of the widespread desire for peace.

SUMMER SCENE in Weston Park (*left*), with two rather elegant vintage push-chairs and an enormous wheelbarrow in evidence. It's all very peaceful and relaxed. The seated ladies are obviously in charge of the push-chairs, but the wheelbarrow is unattended. At that size, however, there was very little chance of it being stolen.

Longley Park open-air swimming pool (*below*), which opened in September 1938, was paid for by Mr George H. Lawrence, well-known Sheffield cutlery manufacturer and benefactor. He also paid for an open-air swimming pool at Hathersage and helped many local charities. Early in the Second World War he and his wife gave half a million francs to the French government for entertainments and comforts for French troops.

Mr Lawrence was tragically killed in the Sheffield blitz, when he left the comparative safety of his home and motored into the city centre to check up on his factory. He was never seen again.

LONDON ROAD was photographed in June 1939 to show some of the property the Corporation intended to buy and knock down so that the road could be widened between Hill Street and John Street. Three months later, Britain was at war and the widening of London Road slipped off the Corporation's list of priorities. It seems it never managed to get back on, because it has pretty much the same unwidened look 50 years later.

Attercliffe had its problems with demolition, too. The vicar complained in 1939 that thirteen clergymen had refused the living before he agreed to take it. And demolition in the area was making it even worse. By then, the old cottages next to Attercliffe Vestry Hall *(left)* looked to be about ready for demolition.

THE COUNCIL for the
Preservation of Rural
England complained in
[19]39 when Parkhead Cottages,
[Ec]clesall Road South, were
[inc]luded in a compulsory
[pu]rchase order and threatened
[wi]th demolition. 'They are
[ch]armingly sited and exemplify
[th]e best of our local building
[tra]dition,' the chairman of
[Sh]effield C.P.R.E. branch wrote
[to] a local newspaper.
'The outskirts of Sheffield
[wi]ll soon be denuded of all
[tr]aces of a style of building
[w]hich might well be used as a
[m]odel for new construction,
[in]stead of the type of red brick
[vi]lla which is rising everywhere
[an]d forming an unsightly rash
[al]l around the city.'
To be fair to the houses on
[K]ents Green Road (right), they
[w]ere not entirely red brick. The
[to]p halves were stucco.

Terminus Rd Millhouses   1963.

IT MUST HAVE been sunnier
in the 1930s. Photographs
of shops taken during the
decade invariably show them
with their sunblinds down, like
these on Terminus Road,
Millhouses. Out of eleven
shops, nine of them have their
blinds down. One even has a
pelmet on it, with the words ;
'Try our noted sandwiches'.
Note that the grass inside the
the old tram loop has been
closely cut and the cuttings
have been taken away.
Nowadays the cuttings are left
where they are to rot.

WHEN Mr Paul Kuenrich, Sheffield steel manufacturer, died in April 1932, memories were revived of a bizarre episode that took place in the city during the First World War.

Mr Kuenrich was born in Saxony and came to Sheffield at the age of 17. He made a successful career in steel and in 1894 became a naturalised British subject. During the war, however, when anti-German feelings ran high, his origins and his name were enough to cause wild rumours in the city. It was said that he was a close friend of the Kaiser, and that he was an important German spy. His house, Holly Court, Millhouses Lane, was said to be full of ammunition and the grounds 'contained concrete beds for the use of guns'.

In an effort to dispel the rumours, Mr Kuenrich invited Sheffield police to carry out a thorough search of Holly Court which they did. At his request, even the pond in the grounds was drained to prove that there were no submerged concrete gun foundations.

At the time Mr Kuenrich's firm was supplying large quantities of materials to the Ministry of Munitions for the British war effort.

Holly Court had another, happier, reputation. The gardens, which were beautifully laid out, were sometimes opened to the public by Mr Kuenrich to raise money for charities.

THORPE HOUSE, Norton Lees, as it looked in the summer of 1932: lawns neatly clipped, borders full, and not another house in sight. The house, once home of the Hall brothers, George and Joseph, later owned by the Cockayne family (of Cockayne's shop on Angel Street), stood near what is now Warminster Road. It was demolished not long after this picture was taken and the grounds were developed for housing – hence the Thorpe House Estate.

The photograph of the two gentlemen and the boundary stone (*left*) was taken just before Norton rural district was absorbed by Sheffield, the idea behind it being to show where the new city boundary would be after the take-over. Just to emphasise the point, one of the gentlemen (the one not wearing spats) is pointing at the boundary stone. No doubt he was pointing on instructions from the photographer. Older cameramen were partial to having people pointing at things in their photographs. It's known as the Glen Baxter school of photography.

Andy White's Celebrities 1937.

Pratt Darnall

NDY WHITE'S
Celebrities,
photographed here
outside Darnall Green Club,
were a junior concert party who
gave charity shows in the
Darnall area in the late 1930s.
For at least two of these young
ladies it was the start of a
career. Evelyn Southern, fifth
along on the right, and now
Mrs Evelyn Smith, and her
friend, Margaret Gregory,
standing next to her on the
right-hand side, both went on
to become profesional dancers.
They were about eleven years
old when the picture was taken,
and 'mad about dancing'.

Reginald Dixon (*right*), born
and brought up in Sheffield,
was 26 years old when he went
to Blackpool one wild and
windy day in March 1930 to
audition for the job of resident
organist at the Tower Ballroom.
He got the job and kept it for
40 years, broadcasting regularly
and playing for millions of
visitors, to many of whom he
was Mr Blackpool.

For the first time in
its 40-year history,
Attercliffe Palace was
provided with a
licensed bar in July
1939. The bar,
costing £1,000,
opened during a
seven-month season
by the Charles
Denville Players.

PALACE THEATRE, ATTERCLIFFE.
6.30   8.45
— Charles Denville Famous Players —
FOR A SEASON OF POPULAR PLAYS.
MONDAY, JULY 3rd, for Six Nights
"The CRIMES of BURKE and HARE"
A thrilling story of the Edinburgh Body-snatchers.
_____
THE NEW THEATRE BAR IS NOW OPEN.

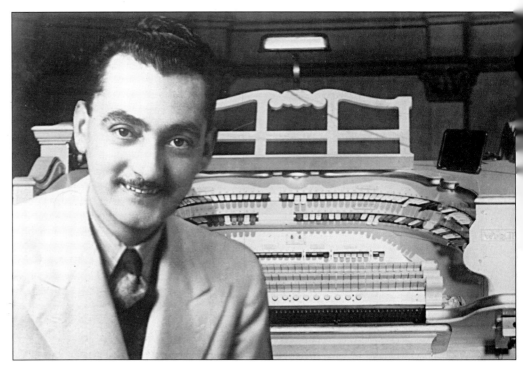

KITTIE AND EDNA, the Prince Sisters, were in the Lyceum pantomime *Mother Goose* in December 1930. Kittie was principal girl and Edna was the squire's son. In addition, said the *Sheffield Daily Telegraph* reviewer, the two of them did 'a risky and attractive specialty turn', singing and dancing. This is them at dress rehearsal and it has to be said on this evidence there is a certain riskiness about them.

In terms of celebrity status, bandleaders were the 1930s equivalent of 1990s rock stars, but instead of touring concert halls and arenas, they travelled the country playing at variety theatres. Most of them brought their bands to Sheffield, Jack Hylton, Henry Hall, Roy Fox, Debroy Somers, Billy Cotton and Harry Roy among them. During their visits they were often the targets of people who wanted famous openers for garden parties, fêtes and suchlike. Roy Fox and his band are seen in the lower photo.

BRUNSWICK CHAPEL, Moorfoot, celebrated i centenary in 1931. Tw years later, soon after the top photograph was taken, land in front of the church was taken for widening The Moor. The lower photograph shows the later appearance of the chapel.

Nothing remains of the building today. After its demolition, St Mary's Gate wa built across the site.

THE BISHOP'S throne at Sheffield Cathedral, designed by Sir Charles Nicholson, was dedicated by the Archbishop of Canterbury, Dr Cosmo Lang, on February 25, 1937, watched by a congregation that included the Princess Royal and her husband, the Earl of Harewood.

Money for the throne was given by the Rt. Rev. John Nathaniel Quirk, Bishop Suffragen of Sheffield from 1901 to 1914. He announced the gift at a farewell party given for him at the Town Hall in 1914, and the throne was dedicated to his memory.

On the day before the dedication, members of the public were given a chance to inspect the throne.

C & A MODES' new store, seen *(left)* just before opening on March 18, 1932, was a handsome addition to High Street. It was built on the site of the old Fitzalan Market, *(below)*, which closed April 1930 after 144 years' business.

The C & A building had a much shorter life. It was destroyed in the blitz of 1940 and rebuilt in the 1950s.

FITZALAN SQUARE, SHEFFIELD.

200819·J.V.

T HE VIEW across
Fitzalan Square before
and after C & A was
built. The *Marples Hotel*, which
was later the scene of the worst
loss of life in the Sheffield blitz,
can be seen in the top
photograph, behind the bus
with an open staircase, at the
top corner of Fitzalan Square.

N SQUARE, SHEFFIELD.

G.235

65

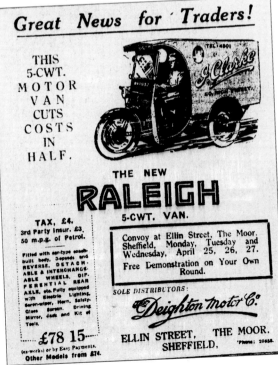

Nowadays firemen sit under cover inside their fire engines when they turn out, and the warning hooter is automatic.

In the 1930s it was different. Some of them stood on a running board alongside the ladder and one of them had the honour of ringing the bell, a much more civilised warning than today's hooter. It was probably less safe riding shotgun in this way, but it was certainly much more impressive for onlookers.

A photographer was on hand when they turned out at Division Street on 13 August, 1936. The picture he took shows the chaps standing on the running board, one of them ringing the bell, and the passers by are so impressed they have stopped passing by.

THERE IS nobody on the running board (right) for this December, 1934 picture of the brigade's new fire engine, ('capable of pumping 1,000 gallons of water a minute'), but that's because the picture was posed. So deliberately posed, in fact, that the seven firemen aboard are looking a mite self-conscious.

Fire engine number 4 (below) dealing with a blaze at Wheldsend's pawnbroker's shop, Langsett Road.

AVIATION was a big talking point in the thirties.

Amy Johnson flew solo to Australia, the Hon. Mrs Victor Bruce flew round the world, two planes flew over Mount Everest, the England-Australia airmail service started, record flights were made in all directions, record altitudes achieved, new speed records established, Britain kept winning the Schneider Trophy...

And Sheffield dithered for the entire decade over whether or not to build itself an airport.

In 1930, the City Council retained pilot Sir Alan Cobham (*left*), head of Cobham's Flying Circus, to advise the city of air facilities. Cobham said, Yes, Sheffield ought to have an airport, and Coal Aston was the best place for it. The City Council agreed, until 1935, when the council changed its mind and decided Coal Aston was *not* the best site, Todwick was better. A year later the council appeared to have gone right off the idea, and passed a resolution saying it was 'not committed' to building an airport. By 1939, when war broke out, it was too late.

Cobham's Flying Circus appeared at Coal Aston several times and at nearby Bakewell, where these four planes were photographed doing a spot of low level formation flying. One of the Cobham team's planes crashed during a visit to Coal Aston, and the pilot was seriously injured.

MEMBERS of Sheffield Aero Club photographed before taking part in a dawn patrol exercise from Netherthorpe airfield in April 1937. The idea was that they had to spot raiding planes coming in from Nottingham, Leicester, Doncaster, Newcastle and Sherburn. The Sheffield flyers could fly at any altitude but the attacking planes could climb no higher than 600 feet. If the registration number of an attacking plane was noted it was it was judged to be shot down and the pilot and his passengers had to pay for their breakfast. If an attacking plane broke through the cordon and landed without his registration being noted, pilot and passengers were entertained to a free breakfast.

Attacking planes had an hour in which to land successfully. Of the ten which landed during the allotted time, six were spotted, so four crews had free breakfasts. Thrills galore were experienced, said a reporter who covered the exercise, especially when one of the attackers came in low over a hedge to avoid being spotted.

Sheffield Aero Club, founded in 1935 to promote an interest in civil aviation, operated a section for the C.A.G., the Civil Air Guard, a kind of airbourne Home Guard.

One of the club planes *(above)* is being wheeled out of the hangar at Netherthorpe in March 1935.

Club instructor, Mr J. Hill, is advising Miss Singleton, a Sheffield member of the Civil Air Guard.

"JOCK" DODDS.
Sheffield United Centre-forward. Season 1938-39.

WALTER MILLERSHIP.
Sheffield Wednesday Centre Half-back and Centre-forward, 1939.

"TOMMY" ALLOTT.
of the Sheffield Speedway Team, 1938.

WITH HIS ample, knee-length shorts, glossy hair parted down the middle, proper leather boots, and shin pads thick enough to stuff the arms of a cinema seat, Ephraim (Jock) Dodds, Sheffield United centre forward, might well be the role model for 1930s footballers.

This photograph, presented free with the *Telegraph and Star* in 1939, will bring tears to the eyes of all United supporters old enough to be convinced that the traditional wide red stripes were best and ought never to have been changed.

Dodds, a Scottish international, was United's top scorer for five consecutive seasons up to his transfer to Blackpool in 1939. He scored more than 100 goals for the club, and in his best season,

1935-36, scored 34.

The picture of Sheffield Wednesday's Walter Millership, given away with *The Star* in 1939, is included to avoid any accusation of United bias.

Millership made 237 league and cup appearances for Wednesday between 1930 and 1945, sometimes as a forward, but mostly as centre half.

The picture of Tommy Allott, given away with the *Telegraph and Star* in 1938, is included to prevent any accusations by Sheffield speedway fans of soccer bias. Allott rode for Sheffield in the 1930s, returned to the Tigers when speedway resumed after the Second World War, and was one of their most consistent performers. His brother Guy also rode for the Tigers.

TEAM CAPTAINS Harry Hooper, of Sheffield United, and Alex James, of Arsenal, shake hands before the 1936 Cup Final. The man in the middle is referee Mr H. Nattrass, of Durham.

The photograph at the bottom of the page shows the goal that prevented Sheffield United bringing the FA Cup back to Sheffield in 1936. Arsenal centre-forward, Drake, the man who scored it, is the one on his knees. Jack Smith, the United goalkeeper, is also on his knees, the ball is in the net, and the Arsenal section of the Wembley crowd is about to erupt.

Only sixteen minutes of the match remained, and before they were over United nearly equalised when their centre-forward Jock Dodds headed against the Arsenal crossbar. George Allison, the Arsenal manager, said later the last sixteen minutes were the longest he had ever known.

DRAKE'S GOAL WINS CUP

ARSENAL'S ROCK-LIKE DEFENCE PREVAILS

UNITED'S DELIGHTFUL CRAFT IN THE FIELD NOT BACKED UP BY ENOUGH FINAL PUNCH

DODDS' WRETCHED LUCK IN BID TO EQUALISE

SHEFFIELD to-day will not house the scenes of wild enthusiasm

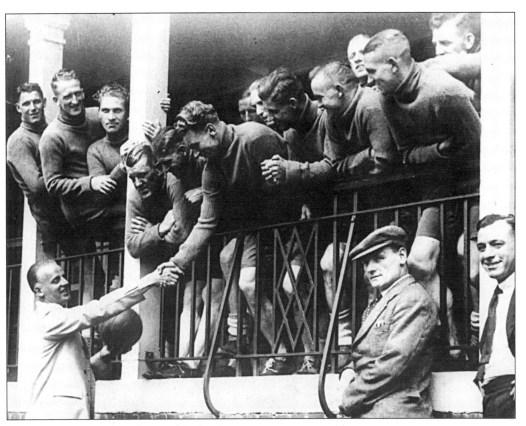

BILLY WALKER (*left*) being greeted by club captain Ronnie Starling and other Sheffield Wednesday players on his appointment as manager of the club in December 1933. Under him, Wednesday won the FA Cup in 1935, but by November 1937 they were bottom of the Second Division and Walker resigned.

He was replaced by Jimmy McMullan, and with McMullan in charge Wednesday just managed to avoid relegation to the Third Division (North)

In the lower picture, Wednesday captain Ronnie Starling is being presented with the cup by the Prince of Wales in 1935.

WEDNESDAY players and directors pose on the Town Hall staircase on April 26, 1935 with the Lord Mayor and Lady Mayoress, Alderman and Mrs P.J.M. Turner – and the FA Cup. It was the last time a Sheffield Lord Mayor or a Sheffield team captain had hands on the trophy.

Sheffield Wednesday outside left Ellis Rimmer is probably the only man in the history of football to have played on the winning side in an FA Cup Final one Saturday, and then appeared in a variety theatre for the following week. Rimmer played for Wednesday in the 1935 final (and scored two of their four goals), returned to Sheffield, took part in the celebrations, then opened at the *Empire Theatre*, playing the piano with two friends, Morrell

and Melville, in an act called Harmony Hotel.

When he appeared on stage the first night he was greeted

with rapturous applause, said one review of the show, but he was nervous and self-conscious. Even so, predicted the reviewer, he would be a terrific draw.

T HE DUKE OF YORK was to have opened Sheffield's new Central Library and Graves Art Gallery on July 5, 1934, but had to cancel his visit because of a poisoned hand. His wife, the Duchess (now the Queen Mother) opened the £142,000 building in his place.

The Duchess of York was shown round the Graves Art Gallery *(opposite)* by Sheffield's Director of Art Galleries, Dr. John Rothenstein.

During the two-day visit she also opened a new outpatients registration department at the Royal Infirmary, and visited Painted Fabrics, Meadowhead, Deep Pits allotments, and Firth Brown's works.

The lower photograph shows her arriving at Painted Fabrics, Meadowhead. Behind the Duchess are the Lord Mayor and Lady Mayoress of Sheffield, Alderman and Mrs Fred Marshall.

At Deep Pits allotments *(above),* the Duchess of York was presented with a stainless steel gardening fork.

Star cartoonist Harry Heap's sketch of the Duke of Kent was published to mark a later Royal Visit to Sheffield, in 1939.

THE DUKE OF KENT

Sketched by Heap, the "Star" artist, on the occasion of to-day's Royal Visit to Sheffield

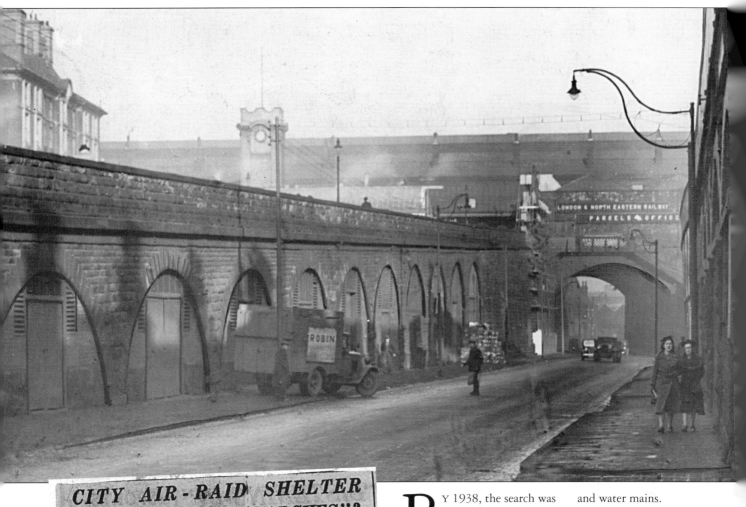

CITY AIR-RAID SHELTER "UNDERNEATH THE ARCHES"?

THE A.R.P. COMMITTEE of Sheffield City Council view favourably a suggestion that the Furnival Road arches, under the Victoria Station approach, should be earmarked for A.R.P. services. The possibility of converting the arches into shelters is to be further investigated.

BY 1938, the search was on for tunnels, cellars, basement storage rooms, mine shafts, and anything else that could conceivably be converted into an air raid shelter in case war came. One suggestion made during the year was that the Furnival Road arches (*above*) under Victoria Station approach should be earmarked for A.R.P. services.

Totley Brook (*left*), in November 1938. The chap waving the rattle is an air raid warden. He is waving the rattle to warn local residents of a gas attack. There hadn't been a gas attack, of course, it was all part of a large A.R.P. exercise covering the whole Sheffield southern division, and involving 1,300 wardens.

Hundreds of incidents were staged, including casualties, gas bombs, high explosive bombs, damage to roads, electric cables and water mains.

As wardens went round their beats they came across warnings of incidents pinned up in prominent places. At Totley Brook Road the warning of a gas attack was pinned to a gas lamp. One snag that showed up during the exercise was that the ten telephone lines to central control at Woodseats police station were nowhere near enough. Otherwise, everything went well.

The odd thing about the photograph is that the warden does not appear to have a gas mask. His assistant is obviously a belt-and-braces lady; she has a large torch in one hand and a small torch in the other. She does not have a gas mask either. Nor does the chap in the overalls who looks as if he, too, is part of the exercise. Perhaps all their gas masks were on the back seat of the car.

JOHN WALSH'S store, pride of the High Street, built 1899, destroyed in the blitz of 1940, is seen here in the late 1930s, in days when an orchestra still played daily in the second floor restaurant. The store boasted three and a half acres of floor space. The small windows on the top two floors were originally restrooms and bedrooms for the staff.

The store was rebuilt in the 1950s, and is now the House of Fraser. To the left of the picture is the Bodega, and to the right, a small piece of the Westminster Hotel. They too were destroyed in the blitz.

War Minister Leslie Hore-Belisha (right) chats with Sheffield soldiers during a lightning tour of defence posts in July 1939.

THROUGHOUT the early part of 1939 there were almost
daily pictures in both local newspapers of anti-aircraft gun
sites and searchlights, all of them described as being
'somewhere near Sheffield', or 'part of Sheffield's defences'. This
searchlight is 'somewhere near Sheffield'. The pictures were a
sustained effort to reassure people. Sheffield, it was said, had a
complete circuit of defence posts.

When Mr Leslie Hore-Belisha, War Minister, inspected some of
them during a 200-mile tour of Sheffield, South Yorkshire, North
Nottinghamshire and Lincolnshire in July 1939, he told a
journalist covering his visit: 'This is a steel city. A most important
city. It is ringed with defences of steel.'

The defences were to be tested all too soon.